A NOTE ON THE AUTHOR

Dr Olivia Remes is a mental health researcher at the University of Cambridge, a public speaker and a life coach. She has researched mental health issues such as anxiety and depression and coping strategies. She is a regular speaker on BBC Radio Cambridgeshire and has appeared on *Woman's Hour* and NPR. Her work has been featured in publications across the world. Her Ted Talks about anxiety, loneliness and coping solutions have garnered nearly 3 million views. This is her first book.

THE INSTANT MOOD FIX

EMERGENCY REMEDIES TO BEAT ANXIETY, PANIC OR STRESS

DR OLIVIA REMES

This publication is designed to provide accurate and authoritative information in regard to the subject matter covered. It is sold with the understanding that the publisher is not engaged in rendering legal, accounting, or other professional service. If legal advice or other expert assistance is required, the services of a competent professional person should be sought. —*From a Declaration of Principles Jointly Adopted by a Committee of the American Bar Association and a Committee of Publishers and Associations*

This book is based on true events, but all persons appearing in the book are either fictitious or have had their names and identifying characteristics changed to protect their privacy. Any resemblance to real people, living or dead, is entirely coincidental.

Medical disclaimer: This book does not replace medical attention from qualified practitioners. Please consult a GP or psychologist before starting any serious course of treatment.

Published by Sourcebooks
P.O. Box 4410, Naperville, Illinois 60567-4410
(630) 961-3900
sourcebooks.com

Originally published in 2021 in Great Britain by Happy Place, an imprint of Ebury Publishing. Ebury Press is part of the Penguin Random House group of companies whose addresses can be found at global.penguinrandomhouse.com

Cataloging-in-Publication Data is on file with the Library of Congress.

Printed and bound in the United States of America.
POD

I dedicate this book to my mom who has not only survived some of the toughest hardships life can offer, but is the perfect example of someone who can bounce back no matter what. She has been the guiding light in my life.

TABLE OF CONTENTS

INTRODUCTION

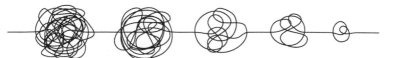

ABOUT ME

I'm a scientist at the University of Cambridge where, for nearly a decade, I have been researching what makes people thrive in life and bounce back from difficult situations. Through my Ted Talks, seminars and discussions with hundreds of people, I discovered that there are 10 types of thinking patterns and feelings – 10 'bad moods' – that keep people from reaching their potential. These moods are extremely common, but if you leave them to fester long enough, they can have a significant impact on your well-being and happiness. Through this book I'd like to help you identify these moods, get past them and bounce back.

ABOUT THIS BOOK

This isn't just a book; it's a package of science-based strategies that tackle key areas of your life: your mindset, social life, work and personal struggles. Based on my research and the interactions with people who have come to my seminars and presentations, I have created a toolkit with coping strategies that you can practise *anytime, anywhere* to become more optimistic, more decisive and more confident.

As you advance through this book and apply these tips and tricks, you will feel yourself becoming more relaxed, like a quiet strength has been born within you. You will feel that life is becoming a daily source of satisfaction, and when this happens, you will feel yourself slowly transforming. I want you to see this book as a 'prescription', with some remedies to use in moments of crisis, and others to take in small doses but which will have a huge cumulative effect. Each chapter in this book is short and will take you approximately 20 minutes to read through. But when panic hits, you may wish to focus on the short-term advice at the start of each chapter, which often takes no more than 2 minutes to read. Use these to shift your mood when the going gets tough and you just need a pick-me-up. Each chapter deals with a different mood so that you can dip in as needed and can go directly to the strategies you're looking for.

These are the 10 moods that I want to help you with:

- Feeling indecisive
- Feeling unmotivated
- Feeling out of control
- Feeling stressed
- Feeling overwhelmed
- Feeling anxious
- Feeling lonely
- Feeling rejected
- Feeling low
- Feeling let down

Each chapter is structured as follows (look out for these icons in each chapter!):

Section 1: Read in case of emergency. This is a quick read of no more than 2 minutes and it'll help you pull yourself out of a difficult moment.

Section 2: Quick science. The background information on the psychology of the moods, feelings and emotions in question. This is a short summary that gives you insights into what happens to you on a psychological and/or neuroscientific level and how other people are affected by these emotions too.

Section 3: How to cope. Long-term strategies to tackle a particular mood or feeling. This is an in-depth development plan for you to build resilience and cope with setbacks.

No matter the hand you've been dealt in life and where you're at now, you will find tried and tested, creative and achievable solutions that will help you.

MY OWN EXPERIENCE

When my mother's cancer returned two summers ago, I felt one of the feelings I'll be talking about in this book – overwhelm – I didn't know which way to turn. Life suddenly didn't seem to make sense anymore and I felt disconnected from the world. I turned to the 10 strategies and practised them whenever I felt low. Slowly, I noticed my own inner strength increasing. It felt like invisible hands had lifted me from the ground back up and I could get back on life's saddle. I wrote this book to show you that there are simple, effective ways for dealing with challenging moods and getting you back in the driving seat.

CHAPTER 1:

FEELING INDECISIVE?
How to make decisions

This chapter shows you how to make decisions and become more decisive. Whether you're struggling with deciding which job to apply for, where to move to, or which shoes to buy, you will discover strategies for making decisions with confidence. It will also help you to make decisions with greater ease and let go of the fear that holds you back.

If it takes you a long time to make up your mind or you've been relying on other people for reassurance or to make decisions for you, this chapter will show you how to turn this around. It's all about how to take control of your life and live with intent.

READ IN CASE OF EMERGENCY

- **Go with your first instinct when it comes to complex decisions.** Researchers at the University of Amsterdam showed that the more complex the decision, the better it is to go with your initial gut reaction. If the choice is a relatively simple one, such as which towel to buy, then weighing up the pros and cons can be helpful. But paradoxically, the more complex the decision, such as which furniture or car to buy, the better it is to let your unconscious brain guide you. And to trust your intuition.[1, 2]

THE SCIENCE OF DECISION-MAKING

Reading time: 10 minutes

Indecision can leave you feeling frustrated. If it's something that happens to you on a regular basis, it can be a significant setback in your life, and it can hold you back in important ways.

Sometimes people struggle with decisions for hours: they spend a long time trying to find the best product, trying to polish their emails to perfection, trying to decide what to order. Sometimes after they make a decision, they're still unsatisfied with their choice, wondering if they should have picked something else.

The way you make decisions can have a significant impact on your life. It can determine whether you get things done or stand still. It can determine whether when you're presented with an opportunity you go for it, or hold back. This chapter looks at how our minds protect us from suffering too much if we make 'bad' decisions. If you've been in an indecisive mood for a long time, there are effective strategies you can use to make decisions with greater ease, strategies to develop intent in your life. This chapter will show you how.

M&S: 'Maximisers' versus 'satisficers'

Psychologist Barry Schwartz found that people can be grouped in various ways when it comes to their decision-making styles. Some people are 'maximisers' while others are 'satisficers'.[3]

You've probably met maximisers along the way or maybe you think you're one. Maximisers are people who make decisions after they've gathered all the information and left no stone unturned. If they need to buy a new coat, they look at as many shops as possible and try on as many coats as they can before making a choice. They are driven by finding 'the best'. Whether that's the best coat, the best laptop, or even the best partner. If you're a maximiser and something breaks down in your home, you might call a tradesperson. But the process you take to find one is often long and difficult: you search all the tradespeople in your area, read as many reviews as possible, browse the internet for hours before you make a decision. This is time-consuming and can sap your energy. Because maximisers have a thorough and meticulous nature, they often put off making decisions and delay action. This is because the process of choosing and studying every possibility is so daunting. Yes, maximisers sometimes find nuggets of gold in their thorough search, but by the time they've found them, they're exhausted. They can't even take pleasure in what they find because their energies are drained.

'Satisficers' are the opposite: If they need to purchase something, they look at a few options and if they find something that more or less satisfies what they're looking for, they go for it. Satisficers are not driven by the need for perfection, and because of this, their lives are often more relaxed. Satisficers go by one important rule that helps them make decisions in life. And this rule is: *good enough*. Because they're not driven by 'perfect', they don't get down if they see something better has come along after they've made their choice. Maximisers, on the other hand, tend to delay making choices, especially if they know they can't go back and change their minds – because what if something better comes along that overshadows what's on offer at present? So in this way, they're always on the lookout for something better. And this can get in the way of their happiness.

The world of choice
If you're a maximiser, it can be hard to live in this ever-changing, materialistic world. Today, we have more choice than ever. All you have to do is go online and see the myriad food products, TV shows, video games, places to go. If you're a maximiser, you're tempted to want to research everything available on the market before buying a product – but how can you do that when there are dozens, potentially hundreds of choices to pick from?

This brings us to an important point: when people are presented with too many options, they tend to fare worse. In one experiment, people who were presented with a smaller selection of chocolate – six types – were more likely to actually buy something than when they're presented with 30 types of chocolate.[4] When people's choices are limited, they're also more satisfied with what they buy.

We see this happening when it comes to work, too. Students asked to write an essay but presented with fewer topics to pick from actually do better on their essay than those who can choose from more topics.[4] As it turns out, less *is* more. When we see less and are surrounded by less, choosing becomes easier. We're more satisfied with what we pick. Maybe this has to do with de-cluttering and living a simpler life, living a happier life in which we buy only what we need and enjoy what we have more.

This is why in a world of online shopping and a bottomless pit of faces on online dating platforms, it may be better to go by the 'good enough' rule.[6] In this ever-changing world in which bigger and better gadgets come along every few months, and people break up with increasingly greater frequency, aiming for 'perfect' is like running towards a finish line that is a mirage. A finish line that just keeps moving away with every step you take forward, a finish line you can never quite reach. The 'perfect' product, house, career etc doesn't exist, because a newer and better one can pop up just around the corner. This is why 'good enough' can save us all from a life of relentless chasing after something that doesn't even exist.

The psychological immune system

People sometimes hold off on making decisions, because they are afraid. They are afraid of the risks that go along with choosing, especially if the choice is a permanent one. They worry that if their decision doesn't turn out the way they hope, they will be affected for a long time afterwards. But what people often don't realize is that we tend to overestimate how bad we will feel if something doesn't work out the way we want it to. In fact, we can recover faster than expected.

Why are we usually wrong when we try to guess how intensely we might suffer in the future? There are two reasons:

The first reason is that when we think about how upset we will be about a future negative experience, we forget that other events will be happening in our lives *at the same time*.[5-7] These events will

Go for
'good enough'
instead of
'the best'.

be competing for our attention and our emotions. For example, if you try to gauge how bad you'll be feeling if your partner breaks up with you in about a month's time, you might predict that you'll be very unhappy. If you were together for years and your relationship was a happy one, you might think that nothing will make you smile for a long time afterwards. Or if you lose someone close to you, you might predict that you'll be depressed and in a consistently low mood for years. But let's assume one of these things actually does happen: your relationship breaks down or you lose someone. There's no doubt that it can be incredibly difficult to go through these periods, but research shows that the intensity of our emotions isn't as high as we might think.[5-7] *We often predict that we'll feel stronger negative emotions to hardship than we actually do.*

This is because many other things are happening during the difficult period that can make us feel good and that *do* put a smile on our face. Maybe you're having a phone call with a good friend, relishing a cold drink on a hot summer day, getting ready for a work event, and all this occupies your mental space and, at times, can even give you small bursts of joy. People who are asked to think about how bad they might feel if such negative events were to happen to them often predict *lasting negative moods*. They don't think about all of the other events that can happen to them at the same time that can lift their moods. It's a human fallacy: we focus solely on the breakup or the loss and our moods around that, while forgetting about everything else. This can keep you stuck. It can prevent you from making decisions and taking a risk.

The second reason why we overestimate how bad an outcome will be is because our psychological immune system is at work.[5-7] Just as we have a physiological immune system for the body, which helps us fight off infections and illnesses, we have a defence mechanism for the mind. When something negative happens to us, we have inbuilt mental processes that can help us buffer the impact of catastrophes.

Daniel Gilbert at Harvard University showed that we have an internal defence mechanism, which can prevent us from getting too down if things don't work out.[5-7] So if we don't get the scholarship or job we were looking for, we might say to ourselves, 'that wasn't what I wanted anyway' to feel better. We start to find flaws with the *very things we desired* so that we feel less hurt. This is our psychological immune system at play. Our minds can go to great lengths to bump up our moods; it can even distort reality. The secret is to not become too aware of this psychological immune system. As Gilbert says, we have to let it work quietly, on its own and without any interference on our part.

But now that we *do* know about this system, how can we all put this information to good use? Next time you have to make a decision and are worried about making the wrong choice, realize that whatever happens and however the decision pans out, you'll be okay – and much more so than you may realize right now. Gilbert's research shows that we're capable of weathering emotional storms to a greater degree than we think,[7] and we should use this ally that we have – our psychological immune system. So if we go back to decision-making, how do we do this?

Instead of basing decisions on fear and remaining on the sidelines, aim to make decisions based on what you actually *want* in life. And don't look back.

If people knew they wouldn't feel as bad while they think about setbacks, they might not try as hard. The upside is that we can put this knowledge to good use: if a decision doesn't work out, it won't feel nearly as bad as you think

We have a psychological immune system that protects us from suffering too intensely in life.

it will.

HOW TO COPE: 5 STRATEGIES TO OVERCOME INDECISION

Reading time: 🕐 10 minutes

We've seen that our psychological immune system can protect us if we make a 'bad' decision and that we should go for it instead of holding back. There are also other strategies that can help you become a more decisive person. Let's go through them:

1. Learn to tolerate risk

Anytime you make a decision, you take a risk. Even if you're deciding on something relatively minor, such as which TV show to watch, you're taking a risk: maybe you won't like your choice. When you're making a bigger decision, such as whether to move to another city, there are potentially even greater risks: will you make friends or find a job? The key is not to push off decisions into the future or not make them, but rather learn to *tolerate the risks that go along with making decisions*.

And why is this important? Because how decisive you are can affect how you see yourself. When people are chronically indecisive and change their minds often, they can begin to lose trust in themselves. Maybe they've decided that tomorrow, they will make a phone call. But then when tomorrow comes around, they decide to put it off and focus on a looming deadline. Changing your mind often and regularly going back on your word can make you lose trust in yourself, it can make you lose confidence that you'll follow through.

This is why it's good to make decisions and learn to tolerate the risks that come with them. Learn to accept the fact that there's an element of unpredictability in life. And the quicker you learn to accept this, the easier it will be.

2. Switch your focus - celebrate decisiveness

If you want to become a more decisive person, it's important to practise making faster decisions. After you've thought about your options for enough time, say 30 minutes, it's important to make a choice. And then after you've made your decision, it's better to *be happy that you were decisive* instead of having made the 'right' decision. When you become happy because you acted decisively, this can fuel feelings of motivation and spur you on to act decisively again in the future.

3. What energizes you?

If you're struggling with making a decision about what job to go for or the direction to take your career in, ask yourself: what energizes you? This can give you the key as to what you enjoy doing, what you find satisfying, what you find fulfilling.

4. ' What would I do if I knew I couldn't fail'?

Anytime you're feeling insecure about a decision - such as whether or not to ask your boss for time off or your partner to spend more time with you - ask yourself this powerful question. The answer can be the key to great insights that you can use to change your life.

5. Push the reset button on your life

I'd like to close this chapter with a thought: sometimes when our decisions don't work out and we're criticizing ourselves for all sorts of reasons, we grind to a halt. We stop trying and taking risks. When

Be happy that you were decisive and not that you made the right decision.

this happens, something that can help you feel better is simply to *push the reset button on our life and start anew.*

When we make a mistake, we tend to keep mental notes of this - we remember. The more we keep tabs on 'poor choices', mistakes and regrets, the more the mental notes pile up. We tend to think that the more we hold on to these notes, the better we'll do next time around. But this doesn't happen. Instead, remembering all the times of indecision, blunders and 'failures' only makes you feel powerless and drains your motivation.

So we have to do something else: push the reset button on our life and start from zero. We have to take a sponge and wipe everything off our mental slate and remove the notes. We have to let go of the negatives. We have to start from day one, today, and from this point onwards adopt new habits and slowly build ourselves back up. Other opportunities will come along, we will find new ways to thrive.

If the last week, month or year didn't go to plan and decisions didn't pan out, wipe away all the self-criticism and start from the beginning. Push the reset button on your life and take the first step forward.

Bringing it all together

Making decisions is something that a lot of people struggle with. Often the basis of this is fear - fear of making the wrong decision, fear of not achieving your outcomes. But paradoxically, the more you let go of this fear and learn to accept that sometimes your decisions won't work out the way you hope, the more decisive you can become. The more you practise tolerating the risks that come with making decisions, the easier it becomes to decide.

If you were to try using one strategy from this chapter now, which one would it be? If you were to start using this strategy for the next three weeks whenever you need to make decisions, how would this change your experience? How would it change your life?

Take the strategy that you picked, write it down and place a checkmark or tick every time you use it. Then write down how your day has changed because of it.

Practise the strategy		
Day	Used strategy? If yes, place checkmark/tick below	How did your day change? Did you feel happier, more in charge, or more relaxed after you used it? Write down any thoughts that come to mind.
Day 1		
Day 2		

Day 3		
Day 4		
Day 5		
Day 6		
Day 7		
Day 8		
Day 9		
Day 10		
Day 11		
Day 12		
Day 13		
Day 14		
Day 15		
Day 16		
Day 17		
Day 18		
Day 19		
Day 20		
Day 21		

CHAPTER 2:

FEELING UNMOTIVATED?
How to get it done (badly)

Are you struggling to begin work on a task because you don't feel like it? Are you finding it hard to get started on a project? Do you feel like you're not ready enough to get going? Whether it's a project at work, cooking or cleaning, having a tricky conversation, people often want to do their tasks well. Perfectly, even. But this need to do it perfectly can cause paralysis and stress. It can cause delays and you might never even begin.

If you need to get started on a task and feel like you are behind, a sure-fire way to get going again is to **do it badly**. The sections in this chapter talk about why 'do it badly' works and how it can catapult you straight into action. This chapter also teaches you long-term coping strategies to *beat procrastination and get motivated*.

READ IN CASE OF EMERGENCY

- **Resist daydreams**. We spend over a third of our day thinking about things that are unrelated to the task at hand.[8] Daydreaming can lead to rumination and make you start zooming in on the goals you still haven't achieved.[9] So, whenever you catch your mind wandering, re-direct it back what you need to do.

THE PSYCHOLOGY OF PROCRASTINATION

Reading time: 5 minutes

The word 'procrastination' comes from Latin, where *pro is* 'forward' and *crastinus* is 'tomorrow'. It's a delay that is often unnecessary and we do it even though we know it would be in our best interest to act now.

So, why do we delay if we know it's bad for us? One reason is that we want to feel comfortable, we want to feel relaxed. We don't like having unpleasant feelings, like frustration or irritation, because of a task. So we do anything in our power to avoid this. While delaying works in the short term because it gives you instant relief, it doesn't work in the long term. Chronic delay can lead to stress[10,11], which can weaken the immune system. It can also lead to regret, because you're not living up to your potential - life becomes a chain of missed opportunities.

Procrastination is also linked to low self-belief[12]: you don't think you can do it. Former tennis coach and author Tim Gallwey[13] worked with some of the best tennis players in the world. He says that our performance in life is equal to our potential minus the interference that comes from negative thoughts and self-limiting beliefs. It's a simple equation:

$$\text{Performance} = \text{Potential} - \text{Interference}$$

People have more potential than they think they do, but this constant interference from their negative thoughts gets in the way. They inhibit their self-growth because of thoughts like, 'I can't do it' or 'I won't get that job'. These thoughts are so powerful that they not only demoralize you, they can also affect your performance in life. But if you minimize this interference from negative thoughts, you can turn things around.

The myth: I'll feel like it more tomorrow
'I'll feel like it more tomorrow' - this is one of the biggest myths when it comes to procrastination. We keep thinking that we'll feel like it more later, even though experience proves to us over and over again that this doesn't happen. The reason for this is that the human mind can play tricks on us; we think that we're pretty good forecasters of our own emotions. We think that we'll be more moti-

vated to work later, but when 'later' arrives, we're still as unmotivated as before.[14]

When you know that the human mind has this flaw – that it's
poor at judging how you'll be feeling later – it's actually easier to
begin work.[15, 16] Because knowledge is power. Since you know
you probably won't be feeling any more energized or happier to
do your work later, you can begin now. You can *do it badly*.

HOW TO COPE: 5 STRATEGIES TO BEAT PROCRASTINATION AND BECOME MOTIVATED

Reading time: 10 minutes

1. Do it badly

After diving deep into the research, I discovered the biggest secret
to getting motivated. I'd like to share this secret with you: do it
badly. When you're faced with a daunting task in front of you and
you don't feel like starting, *do it badly*. When you're faced with a
stressful project, instead of delaying until it's the perfect time and
place to begin, jump right in. Don't worry about trying to do a
good job and don't even think about how it's going to look like as
a finished product. When you do it badly, not only have you taken
the first step, but you're on your way to getting things done. 'Do it
badly' replaces frustration with excitement and it turns your mood
from negative to positive.

People who started using this motto told me that they began
feeling capable, happy. They were getting things done instead
of avoiding them. One of the things I often hear is how adequate

people's 'bad' attempts turn out to be. Whatever they'd done in a rush or without putting in much thought, in fact turned out to be pretty good!

As writer and poet G.K. Chesterton used to say, 'Anything worth doing is worth doing badly the first time.' So, do it badly now, and you can always come back to it later and polish it.

In August 2020, I received an email from Ben, who used the 'do it badly' strategy that he had heard about in one of my talks. He told me that when it came to new opportunities, he used to be 'the biggest time waster on the planet, it was virtually paralyzing!' He had been trying my advice ever since the talk and has been relieved of his anxiety: 'Those three words did what literally thousands of hours of self-help books, self-talk and other actions couldn't do. I've read about "failing my way to success" and every method of "overcoming" my ego, my fear or my anxiety, but just hearing it the way you said it resonated with me,' he wrote.

2. Sit with discomfort

Once you get started, you can develop a habit of action. Do it badly helps you get going and this is a key step. But there are other strategies you can use too, to do things with greater ease, as you'll see in this chapter.

Another strategy is: practise tolerating uncomfortable feelings when you sit down to work. When you put off a task, you do this because that task is likely causing you uncomfortable emotions: aversion or frustration. And because you don't like feeling this way, you want to escape from these emotions. But this can come at a cost, especially if chasing pleasure becomes more important than chasing your goals and dreams.[10, 11] So, instead of running away from your feelings, practise tolerating the discomfort that you get when you sit down to work. The feelings will pass, because they are transitory.

Practise tolerating discomfort when you first sit down to work.

3. Change your focus

During my undergraduate degree, I had many journal articles to read and many of them were dry and complex. In my first year, I would sometimes feel averse to reading the stacks of papers piling up on my desk – I saw them as mandatory reading for my degree, a bitter pill to swallow. It wasn't until I started talking to people about their moods and mental health that I started seeing the meaning behind it all. It wasn't until I started seeing the impact that anxiety and depression can have on someone's life and how powerful coping strategies can be that my view changed. After talking to people about their struggles and mental health problems, I realized that the scientific articles weren't just prerequisites for my job. They held the key to wellbeing, the key to finding purpose and the key to a good life.

I become immersed. I realized that the answers lay in the science. The countless hours that researchers put in to discover how we can take back control over our lives, the thousands upon thousands of participants who take part in their studies around the world. So I read the papers.

I wanted to share this story with you for one reason: when we're faced with a task and simply see the stacks of papers that we have to read, the excel spreadsheets that we have to fill out, we're putting ourselves in a dead-end zone. We impose limits on what we can do. But when you start thinking about *other* emotions you might be feeling at the same time, things start to change. When you take the focus off the boredom and aversion towards your task, and place it on a *different* feeling – maybe the desire to learn something new or an ambition to go up the ladder at work – this can have a significant influence on your motivation. Instead of tapping into the emotions you don't like, focus on the ones you *do* like.

You and I have a landscape of emotions that we can draw on at any given time. This landscape is rich and contains negative emotions, but also positive ones fuelled by desires and curiosities.[14] When we choose to tap into the positive, we start swimming *with* the current instead of against it.

When I focused on the benefits of doing my work, the people I wanted to help, things started to rapidly shift for the better. Nevertheless, there were still days when I found the work difficult. Even if I had a sense of purpose, reading about the same concept for weeks on end could make me feel very frustrated. On the more difficult days, I would take a break and read excerpts from inspiring books. Doing this would re-ignite the fuel within me. It made me remember the meaning of what I was doing, the pleasure of piecing the research together and the joy of finding out something new. And I would get back to my work with a different mindset: a mindset of curiosity.

4. Develop a growth mindset

Another thing you can do to get motivated and closer to the life you want is to develop a 'growth mindset'. Psychologist Carol Dweck studied this aspect and found that people with a growth mindset tend to do particularly well in life. These people see setbacks as opportunities.[17] They don't shy away from problems and instead, they become *more* motivated when they come across something they can't immediately solve.

People with a growth mindset believe that success is a direct result of how much effort they put in. Not how smart they are.

When these people embark on a task, their experience of self-satisfaction depends not so much on the outcome – whether they succeed at the task or if they did it perfectly – but the journey along the way. Sometimes the tougher the journey, the greater their delight.[17] The greater their satisfaction at persisting when it would've been easier to quit. The greater their pride in sticking to it even if they don't succeed.

Ever wonder what people find satisfying when they decide to climb Everest and potentially freeze to death? Or run marathons that make them feel like throwing up? Because they want to feel a sense of pride, a sense of achievement. Because, even though they might not win the marathon or make it all the way to the top of the mountain, they can still feel good that they tried. That they're reaching for the finishing line in spite of the fatigue, in spite of the pain, in spite of the difficulty.

The growth mindset is motivating, it can be fuel for action. When you have the growth mindset, mistakes don't seem such a big deal anymore – they're just a strategy out of many that didn't work out. Trial and error is more important than aiming for perfection.

5. Do 30 minutes of aerobic exercise

Aerobic exercise can significantly boost your level of happiness. Research shows that when you're happier, you become more motivated, and working towards your goals becomes easier.[18] So head out for a walk, dance around the kitchen, put on a workout video, or do whatever cardio you enjoy. This can be a great way to get going again.

Bringing it all together

Whenever you're feeling unmotivated, you can use the strategies in this chapter to catapult yourself straight back into action. Work on developing a growth mindset and put your eye on the mark: what do you want to achieve? **Who do you want to be today?** If one strategy doesn't work out, try another. Instead of aiming for perfection, do it badly.

CHAPTER 3:

FEELING OUT OF CONTROL?
How to strengthen self-control

What is self-control? Any time you put in the effort to think differently, to behave differently, or to feel differently than what you're used to, you're tapping into self-control. Any time you inhibit your urges and direct your behaviour in a deliberate way (e.g. you don't give into distraction and continue working on an assignment), you're tapping into your self-control. And this is important when it comes to going after long-term goals, because it keeps you focused.

Sometimes we don't feel like working for another hour or we want to give into temptation, but we don't give in. We push on a little bit longer or restrain ourselves, because we don't want to make rash decisions or act on impulse. As humans, we don't just behave on autopilot; we have an ability to control ourselves, and the degree to which we're able to do this is one of the key things that makes us different from one another. It's also what gives us flexibility; when we don't act according to impulse, we learn to manoeuvre our thoughts and feelings.

READ IN CASE OF EMERGENCY

- **Wait 10 minutes before you give in.** Whether you're tempted to have another cup of coffee, another cigarette, or surf the internet, wait 10 minutes. This starts to increase your 'willpower', and the 'forbidden fruit' starts to look less tempting. It loses its appeal.

THE SCIENCE OF SELF-CONTROL

Reading time: 🕐 10 minutes

While there are many things in life that are outside of your control, this chapter will show you how to control the things that *are* within your grasp. It will show you how to keep your impulses in check. And this is important because the ability to do this can help you to regulate your feelings and thoughts.[19] Research suggests that being able to exercise control at an early age is a marker of later success in life. Pre-school children who delay gratification are more confident and competent as adolescents and they handle stress better as teens.[20] Children with high self-control are better money-savers in their thirties.[21, 22] It pays to control yourself – both literally and figuratively.

But the good news is, your early disposition doesn't need to define you; your desire to work on self-control is a step in the right direction. Read on to learn about steps you can take towards self-control.

Whenever you try to resist temptation or delay gratification, you're tapping into self-control. It's a strength that allows you to do things that don't come easily to you. Avoiding instant gratification probably feels a little uncomfortable, which is why many of us struggle with it.

When researcher Angela Duckworth at Pennsylvania University was studying self-control, she found that self-control is a better predictor of report card grades in school than innate intelligence.[23] Being intelligent means you're able to learn new skills and learn from your mistakes[24], but self-control is different. It means actively shaping your life in the way that you want to, it means being able to regulate your attention, it means being able to relinquish short-term pleasures in the pursuit of long-term visions.[23]

Your early disposition doesn't need to define you.

People with high self-control also seem to be high achievers, and when we look at them and the ease with which they do everything, it may seem like they're having an easy time and maybe even like they're enjoying it. But this often isn't the case. Psychological studies of 'overachievers' in school showed[23, 25] that self-disciplined students did not necessarily feel positively in the moment. Instead, it was specific goals – getting good marks – that kept them going. If you're not a naturally focused student or worker, this may be reassuring to know. In reality, most of us dislike the daily grind, even if we do it. And those of us who stick it out the longest, win.

Self-control is about a vision that you have and sticking to it in the face of obstacles. And the results bear it out: in studies, students who spent more time doing difficult things, like studying, are the ones who've got more self-control, and these children tend to do well in life.

In our research at the University of Cambridge[26], based on a study of over 20,000 people, we found that it's also beneficial for your mental health to have self-control. We found that feeling in control over yourself and your life can help you make sense of an ever-changing, chaotic world. We looked at data based on women with a strong 'sense of coherence' – these were women who saw the world as manageable and meaningful, they believed challenges were worthy of investing effort. These women had lower levels of anxiety even if they experienced hardship – even if they went through tough times and lived in areas in which most people didn't have a car or lived in overcrowded homes. The women, with a strong 'sense of coherence,' were protected from spiralling downwards when the going got tough.

We also looked at a second group of women – those with a weaker 'sense of coherence'. These women also faced hardship, but contrary to the first group, they didn't perceive the world as manageable and meaningful. They seemed to be missing this sense of control that the first group had. Because of this, the women with a weak sense of coherence had high levels of anxiety when they went through difficulties.

But let's shift gears and take it back to self-control. Below, we look at examples of people who have struggled with self-control and how they overcame their impulses.

We're all going through it

Let me share an example with you:

> Nick is 25 years old. He has struggled with self-control for as long as he can remember. Since university, he'd start eating healthy and promise himself to cut out all junk food 'from now on'. But when he got hungry, all his resolve would go down the drain. He'd tell himself to exercise more, renewing his gym membership, taking two classes and feeling like he was finally doing something about his health. But after an initial burst of enthusiasm, life would get in the way and he'd find it hard to maintain his exercise routine. So he'd abandon the gym, until his conscience guilted him into being more active again a few months later. Every time he resolved to do something, it would only work for a few days before the plan fell through. The problem wasn't his willingness to do things or take better care of his body; it was that he'd set himself goals that were too strict, too difficult to maintain. Either: 'I exercise two or three times a week or I don't do it at all', he says. Either he'd eat only healthy food and cut out everything fried and sugary, or he wouldn't do it at all. The minute he felt tired or his mood would dip, his self-control would fade: his diet would be over and his exercise routine would stop.
>
> The other problem was that the first few days Nick would try something new, he'd start feeling a little burned out from the effort. A little burned out from using his 'self-control muscles' to do the things that didn't come naturally to him.

This 'burning out' of self-control can happen to all of us. Ever notice that when you do something new or go against habits, you find it hard at first? Anytime you use your self-control muscles to do something new or to stop yourself from acting according to impulse, your reserves of self-control strength become a little depleted. So, why is this?

When Martin Seligman at the University of Pennsylvania surveyed over 100,000 people from 54 nations around the world about their character strengths, 'self-control' was something many people seemed to struggle with.[27] While people reported that kindness and fairness were their top strengths, self-control was way down the list. It seems that avoiding temptations is something the entire globe is struggling with. There is some comfort in knowing this, and I hope it helps you become kinder to yourself when you're thinking about your current habits and as you work to change them.

The cost of self-control

Anytime you use self-control, you pay a price. It's a limited resource and if you use it up on one thing, you have less of it for something else. When you put in effort to behave or think in a certain way or not eat that chocolate cake for lunch, your self-control becomes depleted.[28] Studies have shown that people who made themselves resist the temptation of chocolate gave up more easily on a hard puzzle afterwards than those who were able to indulge in chocolate.[29] Abstaining from your favourite alcoholic drink can deplete your self-control and make it harder for you to put in effort afterwards.[30] American researcher Mark Muraven put this to the test with a study on social drinkers, conducted with people aged 21 to 45 who drink at least one alcoholic beverage a week.[30] He gave the participants the following instructions: they were told to place their usual alcoholic drink next to them and to sniff the alcohol without taking a sip. The participants were told that if they really wanted a sip, they could have one, but to try to resist doing so. Then the participants were asked to do tasks. But since they had already depleted some of their self-control because they abstained from drinking, they had a harder time doing the allocated tasks.

Can you guess what happened when, in the same experiment, the participants alternatively smelled water? They performed better on the tasks. One of the outcomes of this study was that the people who had to resist the temptation of alcohol had a harder time doing the tasks than the participants who smelled only water.

So, what does this mean for you? Every time we see, smell or imagine something we like but don't actually indulge in it, this may trigger an internal conflict in us – we want the forbidden fruit, but know we shouldn't give in. Every time you use your self-control muscles to override this internal conflict, you become a little more tired and perform worse on whatever you have to do afterwards. You go into self-control 'debt'.

But, the good news is, there is a way to protect our self-control so that we retain a little more of our energy storage so we don't get tired so quickly. This is particularly useful when you're trying to resist temptation. It simplifies your life so that you can hold on to those precious self-regulation stores. And the strategy is: change your environment. This is one of five long-term techniques to improve self-control, which I detail below:

HOW TO COPE: 5 STRATEGIES FOR BETTER SELF-CONTROL

Reading time: 🕐 10 minutes

1. Change your environment

When impulse strikes and you find it hard to control yourself, instead of refraining from something or restricting yourself, remove the object of temptation from your environment.[31] For example, if you want to give up alcohol, throw the bottle out of your home so that you don't have it around you next time you get a craving.

If you don't want to check your phone messages while you're working, leave the phone in another room; I've done this one many times and it works. Before, I used to work with the phone next to my laptop, especially during my Master's degree – many of us did that. And I found that as soon as I hit a small problem or got stuck on something, I'd reach for my phone to get some relief and have a bit of fun. Just a small break. But sometimes, a few messages would turn into one hour of scrolling, and before I knew it, not just my focus but also my motivation was gone. So I decided to try something else. I started leaving my phone in another room or putting it in a drawer so I wouldn't see it. And because my phone was out of sight, I'd forget about it. I became a lot more productive and it was easier to do longer stretches of work without all those small interruptions. This has been the single most effective (and easiest!) thing I've done to get rid of that phone addiction that many of us have.

The reason that this strategy works is simple: often, whatever is out of sight really is out of mind. When we actively change our situation it's easier to control ourselves. The people that we surround ourselves with, no doubt, influence us. But so do the objects that come into our line of vision daily. Change that thing that is creating distractions or temptation: hide your phone, remove desktop notifications from your computer, remove snacks from your home. Once you do, your environment will support *you* rather than you using up all of your effort to avoid the temptations in your environment.

2. Flex your self-control muscles

The secret is: the more you flex your self-control muscles and use them, the more your self-control builds.[28] A landmark study by Muraven provides the evidence for this. In this study, 69 university students were asked to do tasks that required them to use self-control.[32] These tasks included not thinking of a polar bear for five minutes and squeezing a hand grip. Trying to keep squeezing a hand grip and overriding urges to relax the hand muscles is tiring and requires the use of self-control.

The researchers also tried something else, and this is where the story takes an unusual turn. The researchers asked some of the participants to do various exercises consistently for two weeks. Some participants were asked to change their posture for two

> The things that come into our line of vision influence us. What we focus on, we think about, and ultimately, we want.

weeks: they were told to sit up or walk straight as often as they could. Others were asked to try to put themselves back in a more positive mood whenever they felt low. And others were asked to write down in detail everything they ate each day.

After the two-week period was over, everyone was called back and asked to do the self-control tasks from the beginning of the experiment, like not thinking of a polar bear and squeezing.

This time around though, there was a difference: those who did the exercises showed overall increased strength – they didn't find it as hard to do the self-control tasks. It made them feel less tired when they did tasks that required effort. This increased strength seemed to spill over into other areas of their lives, too. This study shows that when we initially try to control ourselves, for instance, stick to an exercise routine or work on a project in the evening, it's hard. But if we persist and try to increase our inner strength, even through another unrelated activity such as going on regular walks for two weeks, then this can have a positive effect on all areas in our life.

The main takeaway is that in order to build your capacity for self-regulation or self-control, you have to flex this muscle. When we practise persistence on a task when it would be easier to quit, we are building our self-control. We are building our inner resources and we are boosting our inner strength for the long term.

3. Take a dose of positive emotion

Let's say you've got several things to do in a day. Even if you become better at regulating yourself and flexing your self-control muscles, your mood can still take a dip when you have long tasks or many things to tackle and you feel physically or mentally tired. In those moments, you may find yourself in need of an instant mood fix, of a dose of positivity – something that makes you feel positive feelings. When you're starting to feel that afternoon sluggishness, it might be tempting to push through. But instead, science suggests that the best thing to do may be take a short, 5–10 minute break to give yourself a quick reward. Research by psychologist Dianne Tice shows that people who experience a lift in their moods between tasks persist longer and are able to control themselves better than those who don't experience this dose of positivity.[33]

So what does this dose of positive emotion look like? It could be watching something funny and entertaining (in Tice's study, participants watched videos of Robin Williams and Eddie Murphy or they received a surprise gift).[33] A shot of positive emotion can also come from chatting with a good friend, listening to uplifting music, or doing a quick dance.

4. Focus on the *benefits* of avoiding it

When we're thinking about instant gratification, we tend to focus on the benefits of indulging our short-term cravings. A much more effective strategy is to think about the *costs* that you have to pay if you give in. Anytime we try to restrict ourselves from something or 'force' ourselves to act in a certain way, we're struggling to not give into instant gratification. And we're finding it hard to resist,

Positive emotion is energizing.

because we are focusing on the deliciousness of the 'forbidden fruit', the immediate short-term pleasures. Instead of doing this, focus on the *benefits* of avoiding it. So, if you want to drink less coffee, instead of thinking about the pleasure it may give you, focus on the jitteriness and anxiety you might get if you give in, on the nights of bad sleep.

Whatever situations we find ourselves in, the way we react depends on how we perceive those situations. And the way we perceive them depends, to a large extent, on what we choose to focus on. If you focus on the longer-term costs of indulging in something you momentarily crave, you're making it less tempting for yourself.

5. Nip a temptation in the bud

It's much easier to nip something in the bud than to let it grow and *then* deal with it. Take the example of anger: it's easier to deal with anger just when it's beginning to sprout, to step away for a moment to cool off than to let it grow and try to control it.[31]

Bringing it all together

Self-control is something that can be practised and improved. You can build this resource from scratch by using the strategies in this chapter. Even if right now you feel like you don't have much control over yourself, you can change this through the things that you do. When two cars start along a highway and they're very close together, you don't notice any difference in their paths at first. But if one consistently deviates from the other, even if it's by a very small amount, then over time, a huge gap becomes apparent. At first, you might not feel any radical shift within you, you might not feel any change. But after a few weeks of practice, the deviation from your old self becomes greater, and you are on your way to building a new future.

Do you have a project or goal you're working on achieving right now? If so, try to document your daily progress over two weeks by using the table on page 45. The more you work towards your project or goal, the more your self-control will strengthen. A stronger self-control becomes evident when the task starts to seem less difficult and your mood goes up.

Strengthening your self-control

Write down the task you want to tackle. Then, each day, rate how difficult the task seems from 1 (easy) to 5 (difficult). In the last column, rate your mood from 1 (low) to 5 (positive). The more you tackle the task, the easier it will start to seem and the more your mood will improve – this will give you an indication that your self-control is strengthening.

Task:_____

(e.g. walking 10,000 steps a day; working on a creative project)

	Difficulty 1= easy 2 = 3 = 4 = 5 = difficult	*Mood* 1 = low 2 = 3 = 4 = 5 = positive
Day 1		
Day 2		
Day 3		
Day 4		
Day 5		
Day 6		
Day 7		
Day 8		
Day 9		
Day 10		
Day 11		
Day 12		
Day 13		
Day 14		
Review		

CHAPTER 4:

FEELING STRESSED?
How to use the power of humour

Stress is something virtually all of us deal with on a day-to-day basis. Although a bit of stress is good for us because it motivates us to get things done, when it becomes chronic, that's when your health suffers. Stress can cause significant physical and mental health consequences. It can make us feel exhausted, increase our risk for depression, weaken our immune system and even lead to heart attacks. Some people handle stress well and retain good mental health, while others become overwhelmed, become unable to sleep at night, and 'break down'.

Humour can be a real asset for dealing with stress, so in this chapter we will look at ways to use humour to help you bounce back. The 'Science of stress' section offers a summary of what happens inside our brains and body when stress hits. Finally, we will look at five strategies to beat stress.

READ IN CASE OF EMERGENCY

- **Focus on your breath for 5 minutes.** Slowly breathe in and slowly breathe out. As you do this, let go of all thoughts. If thoughts come back to you, don't follow your thoughts or feed them with energy. Gently bring your attention back to your breaths. This will calm you during moments of tension.
- **Use your 'funny' imagination.** This is my favourite thing to do when I'm struggling with someone who's giving me a hard time and stressing me out. When you use your 'funny' imagination, you begin to see stressful problems in a new light and they seem less threatening. You shift perspective. Here is a script for you to try:

    Replay a conversation you've had with someone who stresses you out. Notice how you're feeling – you're uneasy and maybe even have knots in your stomach. Now imagine them wearing a really funny costume, crank up their voice pitch ten notches, and get them to start hiccupping every two seconds. Now, replay that same stressful conversation, but with all of this in: the costume, the funny voice, the hiccups. How do you feel? Doing this exercise takes away some of the negative feelings that you had when you first thought about the individual. And it takes the stress levels down.

- **Meet with or phone someone who's positive, because emotions are contagious**. If you're feeling on edge, think of someone who's positive and makes you laugh and go for a walk with them (if you can't see them in person, ask them to do a 'walking call'). When we're around people who are happy, we're more likely to become happy too, according to research.[34]

THE SCIENCE OF STRESS

Reading time: ⏱ 2 minutes

When you come face to face with a stressor, your hypothalamus – the part of the brain that controls key bodily functions – is involved in various pathways that spur the adrenal glands into action. The adrenal glands are located on top of both kidneys and release hormones involved in the stress response: hormones such as adrenaline and cortisol. These hormones gear you into action when you're faced with danger, and are involved in the 'fight-or-flight' response: your heart rate speeds up, your blood pressure goes up and your blood glucose levels rise. This bodily reaction can help you in the moment, because you become more alert and better prepared to handle the stress. The problem is when the stress becomes chronic and your body is in this permanent 'fight-

or-flight' mode. When you're constantly feeling keyed up or on edge, and you're overexposed to hormones like cortisol, problems can ensue, such as depression or heart disease, and your memory may become impaired.

However, when you turn to humour and start laughing, your stress response can begin to subside. The level of stress hormones like cortisol and adrenaline begins to decline, and chemicals such as endorphins are released. Endorphins are our body's natural pain-killers and help produce feelings of wellbeing.

There are science-based steps you can take to help you to beat stress. The important thing is you have to take these steps each day and on a consistent basis in order to feel the benefits. If, during the day, you're constantly worried or dwell on negative thoughts, this adds to the stress that you're feeling and impacts the kind of sleep you get several hours later. While people talk about sleep hygiene and doing the right things before bedtime to ease us into sleep, there is also 'daytime hygiene' that we have to maintain. In many ways, what you do all day long is equally important as what you do right before going to bed; when you take care of your mental wellbeing earlier on, it's much easier for your mind to quiet down when the time comes to unwind in the evening.

HOW TO COPE: 5 STRATEGIES TO BEAT STRESS

Reading time: ⏱ 10 minutes

1. Use humour as an antidote

One brilliant strategy to deal with life stress is using humour. When we feel stressed, our emotions can be all over the place and we find it hard to cope. Humour is a powerful antidote. It works by distracting you from the problem at hand, even if it's just for a brief instant. Freud said that humour gives you that 'philosophical detachment' from life. When you focus on something funny, in that brief instant you're taking life a little less seriously. And when you do that, the stress loosens its grip on you and you become more cheerful.[35]

In science, this is called 'coping humour.' According to research, when people go through a difficult situation and feel stressed, using humour is better than staying solemn.[35, 36] This might seem counterintuitive; you might be thinking that you need to give problems the seriousness they deserve. You might be thinking that if you're not worried enough about a problem, then whatever you hope for won't manifest. But this scenario takes you down a path that can harm your wellbeing. When we keep worrying and dwelling on our stresses, they become magnified and we feel even more stress. This is why it's important to use strategies like humour to bounce back.

My grandmother turns to humour no matter what she's going through in life. She has heart disease, has dealt with a serious health scare and the death of her husband (my grandfather), but through it all, she still manages to remain positive. She grabs the opportunity to laugh and make a joke, and remains one of the most upbeat, optimistic people I know.

Using humour as a strategy to manage stress promotes mental wellbeing: science has shown that it gets rid of negative feelings and makes room for those that are positive. It also gives us a short mental break from problems.[35, 37] A study by Western Carolina University is a good example.[38] In this research, 84 participants arrived to take an algebraic test and were split into three groups. Before taking the test, the first group was given 10 cartoons to read, the second group was given poems to read, and the third didn't receive anything. Everyone went in for the test. The researchers discovered that the cartoons group performed better than the others. When the researchers wanted to know why this was the case, various measurements they had taken during the experiment

Humour helps you distance yourself from your problems and gives you clarity of mind.

allowed them to see that it all boiled down to anxiety: people who had read the funny cartoons felt less anxious (which is related to stress), and this resulted in them performing better than the other two groups.

This goes to show that when we're stressed out and feeling on edge, we sometimes lack clarity of mind. Indulging in some humour – reading cartoons or watching a sitcom, meme or video, for example – gives us a bit of respite from it all and renewed mental focus.[38, 39] So, try to work a set amount of humour time into your day, such as 15 minutes.

Cracking jokes when you least feel like it – such as when you're stressed out – triggers positive emotions, which in turn contribute to wellbeing and resilience.[40, 41, 42]

What's more, humour can sometimes change the entire mood of a room – you'll know that if you've had a silly argument with a friend or partner, and then managed to make up when someone cut through the tension with a joke. The great thing is that if joking doesn't come naturally to you, you can practise doing this.

2. Work on your type of humour

The *type* of humour we turn to can have a specific effect on our mental health. People who use good-natured humour tend to experience more positive emotions and fewer negative feelings than those who turn to sarcasm or irony. In an experiment by Stanford University, participants were given a variety of negative pictures to look at (e.g. car accidents, aggressive animals).[37] Scientists measured people's emotional responses to see how they responded without any kind of experimental manipulation. Then some participants were told to look at the pictures and find the humour in them in a good-natured, compassionate way, finding the amusement at how imperfect life can be, but without making fun of what they saw. Others were given the pictures to look at and were told to make fun of them, to laugh at them with scorn and superiority. The researchers then measured people's emotional responses again. They found that those who used good-natured humour boosted their positive emotions and reduced their negative emotions to a greater degree than the people who made fun of what they saw. So when we want to laugh at stress and our problems, it's a good idea to use good-natured humour.

There might be an exception to this. Using good-natured humour may be good when we've got deadlines for work or are dealing with unpleasant situations. When we're faced with a traumatic event or a completely overwhelming situation, mean-spirited humour or mockery may, in fact, be very effective. In recounted experiences, prisoners of war turned to this type of humour to cope (aptly named, 'gallows humour'). When prisoners talked among themselves, they made fun of the guards or the difficulties they went through. This gave them a perception of control in circumstances that were very much beyond their control.[43, 44]

If you're dealing with a situation that feels uncontrollable, this form of gallows humour coping can be helpful. It allows us to get a bit of distance from the problem at hand.

3. Look for the puns

Now, if you consider yourself to be a serious person and worry that you can't make others laugh, fear not! Humour coping isn't really about making others laugh by cracking witty jokes – it's about making *yourself* laugh, particularly when you least feel like it, which is also usually when you need it most. It's about creating and maintaining a more relaxed attitude towards life and not taking everything so seriously. When you begin to laugh, often you begin to feel better. Science shows that we can do certain things to feel more light-hearted and allow humour into our lives.

One of the ways to add humour to our lives is to look for things that we come into contact with on a daily basis that can make us laugh, such as puns. Noticing the puns in newspapers or outdoor signs is an easy way to add humour to your days. When you start

We can train ourselves to become more humorous. Scientists call it 'humour training'.

looking for ways to attract humour into your life, you see that it's often possible to do so.[35]

4. Get to know your sense of humour

Listen to, or watch, different types of comedy shows and see what type you like the most – for example, slapstick, dark humour or topical humour related to the news. This can give you insight into your own sense of humour.[35] When you discover what you're naturally drawn to, then keep gravitating towards that. Watch more of those shows that you like. Watch the stand-up routines of your favourite local comedians. Make time to watch funny things like a prescription. Or work out how to be funny yourself and how you can add your favourite type of humour to your life, whether it's by joining an acting club, a laughter club, a stand-up club. Try your hand at being an active rather than a passive watcher.

5. Keep funny things around you

Another way to add humour to your days is to print out your favourite memes or keep toys on your desk that brighten your mood. On my work desk I've got two Smurfs: one has glasses on, is holding a book, and is pointing its finger at me, as if saying 'it's not time for a break yet!'

The objects surrounding us have an effect on our psyche and mental wellbeing. This is why it's good to surround ourselves with things that can make us smile and better yet, laugh!

Bringing it all together

Humour is a powerful antidote to stress. It can give us a 'philosophical detachment' from life, can help you get a bit of distance from the problem at hand, and give you a new perspective. Even if you don't think you have a sense of humour, this is something that can be trained. And it starts with noticing the funny things around you, bringing the humour back into your life. When we start to look for the humour, we realize that often we're able to spot it. And our moods start to change.

CHAPTER 5:

FEELING OVERWHELMED?
How to self-soothe

Do you have emails coming in, reports due, your boss asking to have a meeting with you – and you feel like you're burning out? Maybe you have to raise a child or take care of someone who's sick and you're running on empty.

If you need tips to beat overwhelm now, please go to the 'Read in case of emergency' section, below. The rest of the chapter talks about the psychology of self-soothing: how you can help yourself bounce back during times of overwhelm and strategies for long-term change.

READ IN CASE OF EMERGENCY

- **Get rid of mental clutter.** Information that you get from social media, news, emails, apps pinging … all add to your mental clutter. Information from these sources crowds out your brain space that you need for important tasks. It's like taking a jar containing mud and water, but the water has separated from the mud so it's clear – and we shake it: the liquid in the jar becomes murky. The same thing happens to our minds when we're cluttering them with information from all sorts of places. We begin to not see clearly anymore.

  When you're feeling overwhelmed, set a time period where you don't indulge in distractions – say for two hours. This will clear up your mind and allow you to get things done, which will significantly lower your stress.

- **Do a belly-breathing exercise.** Imagine there's a balloon in your belly and each time you're breathing in, this balloon expands. When you're breathing out, this balloon shrinks. Do this a few times – it can help you breathe properly and relax.

THE PSYCHOLOGY OF SELF-SOOTHING

Reading time: 🕐 10 minutes

When too many things seem to be happening at once and we are overstimulated, this is referred to as 'overwhelm'. Our brains go into overdrive and we feel like we can't cope anymore. Sometimes when you're feeling overwhelmed, you have to self-soothe. In psychology, we think of soothing as when a parent soothes a crying baby, holds it, touches it gently, cradles it and is kind to it.[45] When we feel like we can't handle any more, feel irritated and want to cry, we have to soothe ourselves. We have to pick ourselves up gently and listen to that quiet little voice within us that tells us what we need. To show you what I mean, I will share my friend Clare's house-moving experience:

'The other night I was feeling overwhelmed with how much stuff I still needed to bring over from my old place into my new home. I felt like I didn't have energy and I couldn't move and my mood was low. I was near tears. I had also been eating badly for the past few weeks; pizza, hardly any vegetables and fruit, and thought that because of this, I was low on energy. The sequence of all the things I needed to do was running through my head that night: I needed to sort through and pack up the leftover items, put them into boxes, and so on. I was thinking to myself that I should do as much as possible that evening, especially since everything needed to be moved out of there within the week. But all the stuff that still needed to be done that night was overwhelming me and it drove me to near tears. So I thought that I would turn to people to help me out of this emotional rut. But when I rang my family, they didn't want to hear me complaining about this and when I looked at my

phone to see if I had received any messages from anyone that could brighten my mood, the inbox was empty. I realized that other people couldn't help me out of this emotional rut and I didn't know what to do.

So I said to myself, "just take it easy". I reasoned that I would go over to my old place and do whatever I could and call it a day. I would walk over slowly at my own rhythm rather than rush to get there fast, and pack whatever I could that evening.

Then an amazing thing happened. When I started walking over to my old place, I started gaining energy. And when I got there and started doing things at my own pace, my mood started lifting. Then I kept going and ended up doing everything I had wanted to finish in the first place – but without even meaning to get through it all. I realized that my extreme lack of energy was not because I hadn't nourished myself properly; it was because I had been putting too much pressure on myself. When I lowered the bar substantially that night about how much I would get done, I started gaining all the energy back. That night, I didn't rely on other people to make me feel better emotionally, I relied on myself. People are fickle – sometimes they're there, other times they're not. But it became clear that evening that you can only really rely on yourself – to get you through those times that sometimes seem overwhelming and to make you feel better.'

Clare's story is empowering and the perfect example of what researchers have been saying all along: An effective way to deal with feelings of overwhelm is to engage in 'self-soothing'. When you lower the bar and your own expectations, and take it easy on yourself, you engage in 'self-soothing'. You comfort yourself, much like a parent does to a baby. When you listen to yourself and drop the self-criticism, your mood begins to lift. When you slow things down, you will become more able to keep up.

To show you how you can apply this to your own situation, I've shared a five-step process to slowing down your mind and dealing with overwhelm. The more you exercise these strategies, the calmer you will feel in those moments as well as in the longterm.

HOW TO COPE: 5 STEPS TO MANAGE OVERWHELM

Reading time: 🕐 10 minutes

1. Press pause

The first thing that can help you feel better is simply pause. Not chasing people and reports, not engaging in conversation with yourself about what to do next. But simply pause. This works any time you're feeling overwhelmed because you're behind. And it also works any time you're relentlessly chasing after a carrot that's dangled in front of you: a work promotion at a company that hardly ever rewards its employees, a person you'd like to win over but can never quite reach, a friend you'd like to make amends with.

When we're feeling overwhelmed, instead of running further, we should just stand still. This means not chasing after something, trying to make things work, or thinking about everything that still needs to be done. Just pause. I applied this the other day when I was overwhelmed and felt like I was spinning on a merry-go-round that I couldn't get off: I had begun my morning with a Zoom meeting, then wrote emails back and forth for what seemed like hours, and then had another meeting. Towards the end of the day, I felt like I hadn't accomplished anything. And so instead of trying to jump into my to-do list headfirst without aim, I stood still.

This gave me a sense of peace and the merry-go-round I was on stopped.

2. Focus on your next step

Once you have allowed yourself to catch a breath, you are in a position to start moving again. Ask yourself: out of all the things you have to cross off your to-do list, what is one thing that you can work on right now that will give you a feeling of accomplishment? One thing that, if you spend time on it now, will make you feel like you are taking a *step forward*?

So pick one thing from your to-do list and let go of everything else for a set period of time. No multi-tasking. Put your 'blinkers' on: no thinking about whatever still needs to be done. When you complete it, reflect on what you have achieved. Be pleased that you have done it.

You can use this strategy for each new thing that you want to tackle. So when you're finished with task number 1, think about the next piece of work that will help you get closer to where you want to in life, and only focus on that while letting go of everything else.

3. Sweep away the bad thoughts

When we feel overwhelmed, we have all sorts of thoughts running through our heads. If you want to get peace of mind, you have to let go of these thoughts. It's like cleaning a dirty kitchen that has a lot of dust on the floor; we take a large broom and sweep the dust out. It's the same thing with our minds. We take a meta-phorical large broom and clear our heads of the to-do lists swirling around and the worries and the anxieties. We decide to let go of the thoughts.

As a student, I took a course in pharmacology and there was a lot of information to memorize for the exam. The professor we had had this energizing joie-de-vivre about her. She would condense a lot of information into each class so you needed to keep your eyes on her when she was talking so you wouldn't miss anything she was saying. Before one of the exams, when we were all stressed and trying to figure out how we'd remember all the medication names and their uses, I remember her telling us in a confident tone: 'Do not worry. Worrying will deprive you of your studying strength.' After all these years, I still have that memory of her saying those words in her usual, self-assured way.

When we clear our heads of worrying thoughts and choose to direct our attention to one task and only think about how we can complete that task, we begin to feel better. Lighter. And paradoxically, this gives us strength.

4. Look at the behaviour of the mind, not the contents

A few years ago, a monk came to our university to give a talk. It took place on a quiet Sunday afternoon, and I still remember the stillness in the old room as he was talking. He said that when people feel overwhelmed and their moods are all over the place, they try to deal with the *contents* of their minds. They try to tackle the worries and the obsessions that arise in their minds, one by one, like a sword fighter who slays one attacker after the other. For example, they might get a thought that overwhelms them and they try to 'fix it' then and there: they do anything to make it go away. And it works: their negative emotions subside. But then another troubling thought comes along and they have to do the same thing all over again. Over time, this constant fighting and 'slaying' of thoughts becomes wearisome.

The monk told us that instead of dealing with the contents of your thoughts, you should be looking at the *behaviour of your mind*. There's no point in looking at the content of your thoughts, because the contents always keep changing. When the mind is very anxious or agitated, all sorts of disturbing images are bound to arise, and we feel overwhelmed. When the mind starts to feel calm, the thoughts, images and intrusions cease. So, how do you do that? You have to metaphorically take your mind in your arms, hold it like a small, restless child, and be patient with it until it calms down.

When parents have a restless child, they try to distract the child, give it more toys, show it something new. The monk explained, what the child needs isn't more stuff. What the child needs is *attention*. So when we start paying attention to 'the child in our hearts' as this monk put it, and we *listen*, we begin to calm down. When we sit with ourselves for a minute and realize that the flood of anxious and worrisome thoughts we're getting come from an agitated mind – an *overwhelmed* mind – our perceptions start to change. We start thinking about what we can do to make it feel better. And in a place where we might've felt restless, we begin to feel peace.

5. Be kind to yourself

Often, trying to tackle *everything* leads you to do *nothing*, because you're feeling overwhelmed, you're feeling stressed, you're feeling like you can't manage. During these times, it's important to be kind to yourself – do what you can and then call it a day. This will help you accomplish more than you would have by forcing yourself to 'do it all'.

Let's say a friend comes up to you to tell you about all the things they're overwhelmed by – what would you say to them? You'd most likely show compassion and encourage them to take care of themselves. You would speak with them in a kind, gentle

When you're feeling overwhelmed, focus on one thing that will make you feel like you're taking a step forward.

way. So when you're feeling like you can't manage, do the same thing with yourself. Show kindness and be your own friend.

Bringing it all together

When you're feeling overwhelmed, it can be hard to sleep, hard to take proper care of yourself, and it can be hard to get anything done. But the way out starts with kindness towards yourself: simply pause and allow yourself to catch your breath. Allow yourself to just stand still and let everything fall to the wayside. When you're in a position to start moving again, focus on one thing at a time. The one thing that helps you progress in life. Take it easy and keep it simple. As Martin Luther King said, 'you don't have to see the whole staircase, just take the first step'.

CHAPTER 6:

FEELING ANXIOUS?

How to deal with difficult thoughts

If you've picked this section, you might be struggling with unwanted thoughts: thoughts that make you feel helpless and that you want to block out, but they just keep coming back. Or maybe you think you're a pessimistic person and want to change this about yourself. In this chapter, I've distilled the key discoveries that scientists have made about optimism: what it is, why some people are more optimistic than others and how we can change to get closer to the life we want. This might just hold the answer to living a more optimistic life, and perhaps even a more fulfilled life.

READ IN CASE OF EMERGENCY

- **Get rid of your internal bully.** Words have power, more so than we realize. Every time you say to yourself (or to others) that you're anxious or incapable or shy, you're cementing an idea into your subconscious that you identify with these traits. The way out is to let go of the internal bully and only talk to yourself in a way you'd speak to a friend.

- **Ask yourself: 'What can I do *right now* that will be helpful for me?'** Any time you feel helpless because you can't change an outcome or think you messed up, ask yourself this question. This puts you in the driving seat and changes your focus. When you do this exercise and then come back to the same problem later, you'll have a different perspective on it and your mood will have changed.

THE PSYCHOLOGY OF ANXIETY

Reading time: ⏱ 10 minutes

Sometimes people who have anxiety for a long time think that it's just a part of their personality. They think maybe they were born fearful or tense and there's nothing they can do, which can make them feel helpless. They feel socially anxious so they think they're an 'awkward' or 'shy' person. Or they can't stop worrying about everything that happens in their lives so they think they're a little bit out of control. So they wait for years until they tell someone what they're going through.[46] However, the longer you wait to manage your anxiety, the more it can negatively affect your health and life.

At the University of Cambridge, my colleagues and I researched 'generalized anxiety disorder'. This is a condition in which you're unable to stop worrying about many things going on in your life, so much so that it can become debilitating. Our study showed that those who have generalized anxiety disorder are at risk of several health outcomes in the long run, including a shortened lifespan in the worst cases. Anxiety makes you behave in certain ways, and if you've had it for a long time, it can even change how you see yourself and present yourself to the world. It can 'scar' you. Our thoughts may become like a self-fulfilling prophecy; the more you think of yourself as socially awkward, the more awkward you become. The more you begin to think of yourself as a 'worry-wart', the more of a worrier you turn into. Slowly, over time, you start to embody whatever you fear. It's like a magical veil in a storybook that approaches you and robs you of your freedom to be your-self: at first, this veil lands on the tips of your hands and feet and slowly moves up your body until it envelops you completely. But it's important to know that you are still yourself underneath it all: your true self that brings a uniqueness to the world and a distinctiveness of thought and creativity. You still have your unique way of being that can make others laugh or listen with interest to the stories you tell.

Over time, the more you allow certain thoughts to seep into your mind, like anxiety-fuelled thoughts, the more helpless you may start to feel. So, how do you change this?

Only focus your thoughts on what you are after, not what you want to avoid. When we try to repress unwanted thoughts (e.g. what we want to avoid), they come back to us like a boomerang. For instance: try not to think of a plate full of spaghetti for the next five seconds. If you're like me, you weren't able to do this! Because when we think about what we want to avoid, we are producing a mental image of it. This strengthens our focus on what we don't want. It's the same with anything else. The more you start telling yourself to stop feeling so anxious, the more anxiety you imagine and start feeling. As psychiatrist Carl Jung wrote, 'what you resist, persists'. When we resist a thought, it tightens its grip on us.

After you identify what you want to focus on, put your ideas into action in a way you'd enjoy. When I was writing my thesis, a 45,000-word document, there were days when I just didn't want to open my laptop and stare at the text anymore. But the clock was ticking and the deadline was looming. Every time I thought of the work that needed to be done, I felt this uncomfortable sensation throughout my whole body. Every time I thought that I needed to stop wasting time, it was harder to write. So I decided to change my approach. I began to think only about what it was that I wanted. I wanted to have an interesting thesis, something that would truly engage people while reading it, but I realized that I couldn't do this if I were to stick to the dry style that I thought academic works needed to be written in. I wanted my thesis to be like a gripping novel. So I said, 'to hell with it!' and decided to change my writing style. For the first time, I began having fun writing my thesis. I became efficient. I wrote half a chapter in one day. Then I started writing other chapters and before I knew it, the thesis was done. There were days when my old thought patterns fuelled by fear would come back and I would revert to the old style. Sometimes I would worry, 'What if my examiners don't like my thesis? What if they don't give me my degree or what if I've made a mistake doing this?' But I did it anyway and it felt good. It felt good because I did it in a way that *I* very much enjoyed.

Thinking only about what you want and doing it in a way that you enjoy can decrease your feelings of helplessness. It's a powerful technique because you get to focus solely on what you want to achieve and let go of the rest. For example, only do exercise routines that you enjoy instead of the ones that you think you *should* do – e.g. if you don't like running, try dancing.

How optimism can help

Another strategy that can help you any time you're dealing with unwanted, negative thoughts and want to boost your mood is becoming more optimistic. We've all met optimists in our lives. These are the people who tend to see the good in the things around them and are hopeful that their problems will work out.[47] They tend to notice and remember the positive. A woman I once met, Elaine, was the definition of an optimist: whatever you saw as a setback, she'd see as an opportunity. If you complained about having too much work, she'd see it as a compliment that your boss relies on you so much and trusts you. If you complained about your neighbour, she'd point out the good things the neighbour does for you. If you were disgruntled about wasting time preparing for a job that you didn't get, she'd say that you've learned something new and every bit of knowledge can help you in the future.

So what is the secret that optimists like Elaine have? They have what psychologists call an 'internal locus of control': they believe they can actively shape their lives through the actions they take.[47] And this can neutralize feelings of helplessness.

Optimists and pessimists differ in how they think about failure. If pessimists fail at something, they see it as a poor reflection on themselves, and make generalizations that cause them to despair over their whole lives. For example, if they make a mistake, they might say something like: 'things are never on my side'. Optimists won't make these generalizations. Instead, they see blunders as something temporary that have nothing to do with them as individuals. They might say 'that strategy wasn't great, I should try a different one next time'. Because they're not harsh with themselves, they're motivated to try again.

Since optimists have this internal locus of control and think they're in charge, they tend to bring an energetic, problem-solving approach to life.[48] They look at what needs to be done and get going. By contrast, the journey of the pessimist is tainted with hesitation and passivity.

Being optimistic not only helps you have a different experience of life, it might also be good for your health. In a study of people with HIV, those who were optimistic showed a slower disease progression. So optimism is correlated with a slower progression of illness.[49] Research on patients with chronic pain showed that pessimists were more likely to succumb to the pain they were feeling and allowed it to take over their lives. The people who were more optimistic felt the pain, but carried on with their activities in spite of what they were feeling.[50] Of course, how much you can do or whether you're able to do anything at all depends on the illness you've got and the symptoms you're experiencing. The point is though, that how we look at problems can enable us to lead our lives one way or another; being optimistic can help.

HOW TO COPE: 5 STRATEGIES TO BECOME MORE OPTIMISTIC

Reading time: 10 minutes

So if you think you're a pessimist or are surrounded by pessimistic people that are bringing you down, is there anything that can be done? Can you become more optimistic? And how do you overcome the hesitation that might be holding you back and take action with greater ease?

1. Be driven by goals, not moods

Pessimism can be tied to fear and anxiety. Because pessimists are driven by their moods, and their hesitations, they tend to slow down and stop. This is why it's important to take actions that are goal-directed, not mood-directed. When people are feeling pessimistic, it is hard to take action. Despite what you may be feeling inside, take a look at where you want to get to in life and plan your actions according to that. When we do the opposite and plan our actions according to fears and anxieties, we tend to hold back, which might not be in our best interest.

The problem of allowing the mood you're in to drive your behaviour is that you might not take any action until you feel motivated, until you're in the 'right' mood. This means waiting to feel energized on the inside, before engaging.[51, 52, 53] But in order to overcome passivity and the moods holding you back, engage in activities that help you reach your goals, despite what you may be feeling on the inside. This can help you set your wheels into motion again, and the first glimmer of hope and optimism can appear again.

2. Reduce your jealousy triggers

How optimistic you're feeling can be determined by the people you come into contact with. Sometimes you may come across a person that you think is more successful than you are. You notice that you feel anger towards them without any specific reason, a sense of resentment. Your mood may take a plunge. You don't exactly know why you don't like them, but they get on your nerves for almost being too perfect: maybe they found a great partner, they have a better job, a nicer home.

People sometimes start feeling negative towards someone when that other person has a personal quality that they would also like to have. Maybe the other person is making you realize that you could have done more with your life 'if only you would've applied yourself a little more or put yourself out there'. And this is causing you pain.

Whatever your reasons, you avoid this individual, because you want to get away from the pain. Why not try another strategy? See how you can use this scenario to your advantage: can you learn from them? This takes much more courage than despising them. There's a reason that this person has come into your life now: it often means that it's not too late to make different life decisions and take action. Use these people as sources of inspiration rather than something that can bring you down. This means being optimistic and seeing the bright side of life.

3. Spend less time around pessimistic people

Sometimes we encounter people that put a damper on our moods: maybe it's a friend, a co-worker, or yes, even a family member. You tell them how excited you are about a new piece of clothing you bought and they say, 'wow, did you need another coat?' These people bring you down little by little and they can make you feel like there's no point in even trying in life. Because there are just too many obstacles in the way. Often they say that the only reason they're saying these things is to help you see things more realistically.

It's likely to be better for your own wellbeing to spend less time around people like this – people who clip your wings – because emotions are contagious. Constantly spending time around people who see the problems, the obstacles in life, may influence you in a negative way. It can take away from your motivation to try new things.

4. Ask yourself this essential relationship question

This tip goes hand-in-hand with the one above. The people we choose to spend our time with may treat us in certain ways, which negatively influence our optimism levels. Maybe you're with someone who criticizes you ever so subtly; maybe they correct your grammar or laugh when you don't know something. You might like spending time with them, but on several occasions you're left feeling *lesser than*. The worst thing you can do is try to change yourself into what you think this person would like you to be. Maybe you fix one 'shortcoming', but then something else pops up … and little by little, you're changing who you are as a person. This can seriously affect your self-esteem and chip away at your sense of optimism.

A test to find out whether your partner or friend is chipping away at your optimism is to ask yourself this: do you feel energized, more attractive and funnier when you're around this person or do you feel like you're not good enough? If you feel like you're broken, it's important to realize that the blame shouldn't be placed on you – but rather on the other person for treating you this way. Someone who is worth knowing treats *everyone* with dignity and respect.

5. Energize your day

This is about infusing your day with something that boosts your mood, that energizes you. For example, wash your hair, try a new hairstyle, go for a run – even though it sounds simple, doing something small like this makes you feel better about yourself, it invigorates you. It's a brick you're laying down on the road to self-esteem and on the road to optimism.

Bringing it all together

If you asked the average person you'd meet on the street whether they'd like to be a pessimist or an optimist, the answer would be simple. Most of us would like to be the optimist: the person who sees the positive side of things, who sees the glass half full. It's not so difficult to become one. It's about practising the strategies you've read about in this chapter one by one, in your own time – because optimism is something that can be trained. When you spend more time around people who treat you well, when you treat *yourself* well, this is not only the road to higher self-esteem – but also to optimism.

CHAPTER 7:

FEELING LONELY?
How to have happy relationships

If you're feeling lonely and want to connect with other people, this chapter has strategies based on science that can help you achieve that. Strategies that can help you see the world through a different lens, beat loneliness and form better connections.

READ IN CASE OF EMERGENCY

- **Talk to one stranger today.** We underestimate the effect that talking to strangers we encounter in our day-to-day can have on us: a neighbour, someone out walking their dog, the person in the coffee queue. When you start talking to other people, even if they're strangers, this can be an instant mood fix. Not only that, but in experiments, people who are taught to 'act extroverted' start feeling more positive.[54]

THE SCIENCE OF LONELINESS

Reading time: ⏱ 10 minutes

Loneliness is something many people are suffering from. Before 2020, about one in five people in the UK were lonely and the pandemic has made this even worse.[55, 56, 57] But what is loneliness? It is the discrepancy between the number and quality of relationships that you would *like* to have and what you *do* have. You can be surrounded by many people and still be lonely – this is why people can be lonely in a marriage or in a crowd. By the same token, you might only have one or two friends, but if your bond with them is strong and your social needs are met, then chances are, you're not lonely.

The researcher John Cacioppo said that the discomfort you get from loneliness can be the same as that from hunger, thirst or physical pain.[58] Human beings are social creatures and without connection, they can break down mentally and physically. Chronically lonely people are at higher risk of early death and their immune system can become suppressed.[59, 60]

Being lonely as a child can have effects well into adulthood. Research shows that if you feel isolated as a child, then you're more likely to have poorer health as a young adult. A study showed that children who spent a lot of time alone and who were not well-liked by their peers had poorer physical health as adults.[61] This is because loneliness can be stressful for the body and being in a chronic state of stress can cause your physical health to deteriorate.

Why does loneliness hurt so much?

Humans have been built in such a way that if we're lonely for too long, it hurts, and if we don't do something about it, we can become sick. And this is all because of evolution. If our early ancestors were on their own for too long, this could represent risk and they could be in danger of being attacked. But if our ancestors were part of a group, they were more protected from danger. This basic instinct for having people around us so that we feel safe has not changed. Therefore, as much as hunger prompts us to get food and thirst prompts us to find a drink, loneliness spurs us into action to find friends. We all have a need to belong, and if this need is not met, we start to feel the adverse effects.[61]

Loneliness affects your thinking

When we're lonely for too long, we begin to feel unsafe, because of our evolutionary survival mechanisms. We start to be on the lookout for threats. In our modern society, the threats are no longer other attackers or animals in the jungle. They're much subtler – they can be the unfriendly expression of someone on a Zoom call or an ambiguous social situation that's making you feel uncertain.

If you're lonely, you're more likely to interpret someone's neutral facial expression as negative and you might think they don't like you. According to research, lonely individuals have a bias for social threats in their environment, expect to be rejected more often, and evaluate themselves and those around them less favourably.[65]

People who are lonely also tend to be less refreshed after a night's sleep even if they got the recommended hours of shut eye.[58] And this can lead to reduced energy the next day, which makes the pain of social isolation even harder to bear, in a vicious cycle.[58]

It's important to understand the full impact of loneliness, because this can be the wake-up call we need to change our lives. Loneliness isn't something trivial. Making friends isn't just a perk. It's necessary for our wellbeing and health.

Did you know that we're less likely to put in effort to do the things that are good for us when we're not satisfied with our social lives? And why is this? It seems that it all comes down to self-control/self-regulation.[66]

Loneliness and self-regulation

When we're lonely, our ability to regulate ourselves goes down. We control ourselves less, so, for example, we're more likely to reach for unhealthy food instead of sticking to a healthy diet, and we tend to give up faster when faced with a challenging task.[66]

Researchers in the US devised an experiment to test this. They wanted to see whether being rejected by others affects how we behave. They recruited university students and told them that they should make an effort to mingle and learn each other's names. The researchers then told everyone that after twenty minutes was up, they would be divided into groups, and this would be done based on who liked who: the students that wanted to work together would be put in the same groups.

So after the mingling and meet-and-greet was over, the experimenters asked the students to write down the names of two people they wanted to work with. The researchers then divided the participants up. But they didn't group the students together based on their preferences or 'who liked who' as they said they would do; instead they allocated randomly. Some students were told by the researchers: 'I have good news for you – everyone chose you as someone they'd like to work with. But we cannot have a group of five (or four, or six) people, so I'll have you do the next task alone.' And they picked others to tell them: 'I hate to tell you this, but no one chose you as someone they wanted to work with. So I'll have you do the next task alone.'

They then gave all the students a task and placed a bowl of cookies next to them. What the researchers saw was that the students who had been told that they were rejected by the others (no one wanted to work with them) ate almost *twice* as many cookies as the students made to feel accepted. The students who were 'rejected' not only ate more cookies, but they also thought the cookies tasted better.[66]

So, why was this happening? One theory is that when we feel like we're being rejected, we have a harder time with self-regulation. We're more likely to skip our exercise routine, or have a harder time stopping ourselves from drinking; we 'let go' a little. The students in the experiment who felt accepted not only ate less, but they seemed to be less consumed with the flavour of the cookies. But it appears the students in the rejected group felt like they were 'starved'. They were starving for connection and needed to feel wanted. Sometimes, when we can't find the comfort we're looking for in other people, we turn to the things in our environment to fill the void, whether it's food, alcohol or our phones.

When we talk to others, our experience changes.

THE SCIENCE OF TALKING TO OTHERS

When we talk to others, our experience changes. University of Chicago researchers[62] asked people how they would feel if they chatted to a fellow passenger on their morning commute instead of keeping to themselves. Even though most believed that striking up a conversation would make for a less pleasant ride, the opposite happened, when they tried it in an experiment. When the experiment rolled out, participants who were randomly assigned to strike up a conversation with their fellow travellers ended up having the most positive journey experience.[62, 63]

So, if we feel better talking, why do we often choose to sit in isolation when we're commuting? Because as the authors of this study say, we 'underestimate others' interest in connecting'[62]. On the bus, on the train, wherever we are, we interpret other people's silence as unwillingness to connect. We see it as disinterest. And so we back off.[62, 63] Even though this experiment was first carried out with Americans, similar findings emerged when the study was replicated in the UK. 'The thing we are crystal clear on in our analysis is that the Brits in our experiment enjoyed talking to strangers just as our American participants did,' said Nicholas Epley, lead researcher of this experiment.[64]

The question is, do we over-indulge in comfort food or get into bad habits when we're lonely because we're incapable of restraining ourselves? Does loneliness cause some kind of permanent switch in your brain that makes you unable to control yourself? Or is there something else at play here? What research shows[66] is that if we're lonely, most of us *do* have the capacity to control ourselves. It's just that we are often less will-ing to. You can restrain yourself, but there is less incentive to do so.

In the US experiment, the researchers saw that the students who were made to feel rejected had a harder time controlling themselves and ate more unhealthy cookies. But the researchers wanted to know, if participants are incentivized in some way, would that make a difference? It turns out that it would. When participants in another experiment conducted by the same researchers were incentivized with cash, they were able to exert self-control. This is important, because when we become aware of something, *we can take steps to redress the situation*.

When we're lonely, we see the world differently

When people are lonely, they ask themselves why they're feeling so lonely or why nobody wants to talk to them. The answers they give themselves can have a significant effect on how they feel and the action they take. It can determine whether they take steps to overcome loneliness or stand still.[67]

If you're asking yourself why you're lonely and the answer you give yourself is that you're not putting in enough effort to go out, this can be motivating. It can make you more willing to fix the situation. You start seeing it as something within your control. In research studies, people who believed that forming new rela-tionships was something within their capacity to change tended to be more social and less lonely. And the reason for this is simple: the more we see our circumstances as within our control, the more we believe we can influence our outcomes through our actions.

On the other hand, if you think that you're lonely because of something that's beyond your control, such as how likeable you are or your luck in life, this can make it difficult to change anything.

If you think that you're awkward and that no matter what you do, people still won't like you, then this creates a perception of uncontrollability because there's something 'wrong' with you.[67]

If we take all the evidence from science and pull it together, we see that loneliness often has to do with our own views. And perception is something that can be changed. Let's look at how:

HOW TO COPE: 5 STRATEGIES TO OVERCOME LONELINESS

Reading time: 10 minutes

1. Focus on what you're doing, not who you are as a person

If you want to overcome loneliness, it's important to realize the power of perception. When you keep asking yourself why no one wants to spend time with you, or tell yourself that 'you're weird,' this creates a mental block. Since you are blaming yourself for the situation, you're subconsciously telling yourself that there's nothing you can do; the problem is 'fixed'.

Instead, start focusing on what you're *doing*. Focus on what you are doing to improve the situation, the steps you're taking to improve the loneliness, e.g. the number of people you spoke to today, joining a new group, club or online community. Research shows that people who do an inventory and look at what they were doing to combat their loneliness are more likely to get back out there and persist.

And this is empowering for the following reason: when we start letting go of the negative perceptions of ourselves, we can begin to focus on our actions. Actions to get ourselves out of the rut we're in and to feel connected to others again.

Having friends isn't just a perk. It's necessary for our health.

2. Accept that everyone reacts differently

Another thing that can help us overcome loneliness is to realize that everyone reacts differently. In order to build connections, you have to accept that people's reactions are and will be different. Some people won't feel the same joy as you when you share good news, and even if you've helped them in the past, they might not return the favour. People's responses are unpredictable and you have to learn to accept this without taking it personally. When you become less affected by other people's reactions, their facial expressions or underwhelming response to your kind gestures, you gain a sense of independence. And often, this independence becomes the very thing that draws other people to you.

We've all heard the advice that if we want to make friends, we should ask other people questions and show interest. This can be a good starting point. But what do you do if the person reacts in a lacklustre way? This can be discouraging. This is why we have to accept that people's reactions are unpredictable and we have to learn to tolerate this aspect.

3. Change the way you listen, not the way you talk

When somebody is talking to us, we're often thinking of what we're going to say next, of our own reply. This prevents you from fully listening and taking in what the other person is saying. This can mean that the other person doesn't really feel 'heard', which means it is hard to truly get to know each other. So, to take your relationships to another level and create better connections, listen with the aim to understand – not with the aim to reply. When you listen to understand, your relationships change and the other person feels heard. When we let go of your own internal thoughts and focus completely on the other person, they begin to feel understood. They begin to feel a connection with us and they begin to feel closer to us.

4. Shift the focus

The more we think about how lonely we are, the worse we feel. One way to overcome this is to shift the focus. Shift the spotlight off yourself and the problems you're struggling with and move the focus onto another person. For example, start thinking of what you can do for someone else, whether it's by volunteering or making a meal for your neighbour or friend who's going through a stressful time. When we devote some time in the day to somebody else, two things happen: first, we distract ourselves from our own problems and the pain of loneliness starts to subside. And second, we start to see that we can make a difference for somebody else. And this improves our feelings of wellbeing.

5. Practise feeling good on your own

Sometimes loneliness isn't just about being around more people. While being around others can make you feel good, it's often not enough. For example, you can go to a party or a meet-up and feel better while you're there, but the moment you're back home, your mood nosedives again. This is why we have to learn to feel good when we're by ourselves too, when nobody's there and we're surrounded by silence.

Bringing it all together

Loneliness is difficult to endure, but you can take steps to beat it. It can start with letting go of questions such as 'why am I so lonely?' and 'why don't people like me?' This is essential because the questions you ask yourself, the words that you say to yourself, have power. They help shape your sense of self, the way you see yourself. If you want to overcome loneliness, you have to focus more on the things you're *doing* rather than who you are as a person. When you take steps to talk to new people, when you take the risk to open up to someone, when you go up to that person and say hello even though it is hard for you, this can give you a feeling of hope. It can help you overcome loneliness and bounce back.

CHAPTER 8:

FEELING REJECTED?
How to get over heartbreak

Maybe you're going through a breakup or a divorce and are look-ing for ways to cope, to deal with the hurt. If you're looking for tips to use urgently, please check 'Read in case of emergency', below. The next section focuses on the psychology of heartbreak: how the explanations you give yourself for the breakup can either boost your self-esteem or drive you into self-loathing. The last section gives you five strategies to help you get past the heartbreak – strat-egies to help you move on, look to the future and feel a sense of possibility again.

READ IN CASE OF EMERGENCY

- **Call someone and talk about something *other* than the breakup.** When we're suffering, an effective way to switch our minds away from the pain is to engage in a different activity. But not just any activity – giving someone a phone call and talking about something other than the breakup can be an instant mood fix. This works because you have no choice but to focus on the conversation. Whether they are talking about cooking, their nieces or a movie, you have no choice but to pay attention so that you can respond. This can put you in a different mental space.

- **Advance on a task.** Even if it's just 30 minutes of tidying the kitchen or tackling a work project. If you don't feel like en-gaging in anything because you're down, when you start doing something that makes you feel like you're *moving forward*, this can help you shift perspective. You will start to see problems more clearly.

- **Wash your bedsheets.** Washing your bedsheets can feel like a life reset. That clean, fresh feeling of getting into a bed that's just been covered with clean sheets is one of the best. Even if a clean bed won't make your problems go away, when you engage in this small act of self-care, you begin to *feel* differently about yourself – better. And this is important at a time when your self-esteem might have taken a bruising.

THE PSYCHOLOGY OF HEARTBREAK

Reading time: 🕐 10 minutes

A breakup or a divorce can be one of the hardest things in life and can really mess with your mood. Whether you're feeling rejected or you initiated the breakup, a split can lead to anxiety and depression, as well as self-destructive behaviours, such as binge drinking.

How much you suffer after a breakup can depend on a few things. It can depend on how much effort you put into trying to be with this person in the first place, how much you tried to 'win them over', and how committed you were to each other. The more effort you put in and the tighter the bond between you two, the harder it can be to let go.[68]

While splitting up is hard to bear, the explanation you give yourself for the ending can have a huge impact on your mental wellbeing. It can either boost your self-esteem or drive you into self-loathing.

The explanation you give yourself for the breakup or divorce can have important consequences for you.

Researchers at Harvard[69] studied divorced women and they saw that these women thought about their split in one of two different ways:

Person attributions – your fault or my fault

Some women used 'person attributions' to explain the end of their marriage: for example, they blamed the other person for the problems they had and saw it as a one-sided situation. But focusing exclusively on yourself and the 'faults' that you have is not a good idea either. If you think that it's only *you* to blame for the split, this can place you on a loop of endless self-criticism. Placing the responsibility for a split on your partner *or* yourself can lead to self-recrimination or resentment and it can harm your self-worth. This is because you feel you can't do anything about it.

Interactive attributions

Other women in the Harvard study used a different type of explanation for their divorces: they used 'interactive attributions'.[69] They realized that their marriage problems weren't necessarily the fault of one person; instead, these women looked at the *interaction* with their partners – they saw their marriage as having broken down because of things like a lack of communication or closeness, or changing lifestyles or values.

Using an 'interactive attribution' to explain your split is more complex and requires more thought than simply blaming yourself or the other person. It's often more realistic and helpful to think about how your interactions led to problems, and this can give you a greater feeling of control.

Sometimes, the problems stem from a mismatch in how you see things or the way you're both communicating. Researchers at Harvard showed that the women who used interactive attributions tended to have higher self-worth than the women who blamed their ex-partner. When the researchers followed these women over time, they saw that the ones with the interactive attributions also turned out to be significantly happier and had more positive feelings towards their ex-husbands than the others.

When we blame someone else for what's happened in a relationship, it might feel 'easier'. Our brains don't have to work as hard to understand and make sense of the situation. Although this can be more convenient in the immediate moment, thinking like this can hurt you in the long run. People who consistently blame the other partner tend to be sadder after the breakup and may be less optimistic.[70] On the other hand, when you take time to work out the reasons for your issues and look at how the interaction between the two of you didn't work, this can help you see the situation more clearly and even shield you from further suffering.

Growing after a breakup

If we go back to the science, we see that breakups and divorces can affect us on a deep level and tamper with our self-esteem. But there are things we can do to bounce back.[71] There's a concept in psychology called 'post-traumatic growth' (see also, chapter 9). Any time we go through something very difficult in life, there's no doubt that our moods can take a real bruising and we can feel distressed. But when we manage to endure it, we can also grow. There are countless stories of people going through some of the toughest times, like cancer or an accident, who have experienced this post-traumatic growth. It's as the saying goes: what doesn't kill you really does make you stronger.

If we apply this to breakups, the same thing can happen. Songs and movies tend to depict breakups as tragic, but what is often not talked about is[72] how difficult situations, like a breakup, can be the springboard you need to start living your life differently – perhaps more meaningfully.

A breakup can lead to increased feelings of independence and can be a chance to rediscover yourself. This is especially the case if you were stuck in a low-quality relationship that didn't allow you to grow.[72] If you're in a relationship now that's making you suffer and the moments of happiness are few and far between, and you're considering ending it, there are a few things to think about:

- Usually, whoever initiates the breakup tends to suffer less.[68] Therefore, if you feel like someone is taking advantage of you or not reciprocating your feelings, it might be easier if you're the one to end things than wait until the other person makes the move.
- If you're going through a divorce and are worried about how you'll fare and what this means for you, there's research evidence to show that men might be happier in marriages, but after a divorce, men are the ones who may feel more distressed. This raises the possibility that women may experience more self-growth than men after a divorce. This can give the many newly-single women in this world hope that being on your own again isn't something to be feared; in fact, it can open up new avenues for you.

My next-door neighbour had been married for twenty years, and when her husband came home one day to tell her that he was leaving her and their two teenage kids for a much younger woman, she was devastated. She hadn't been employed in over twenty years, because he had been the sole provider, and she was fearful to start a new life on her own. I ran into her two years later. She was wearing a trendy workout outfit, holding a bottle of water in one hand and power-walking with her friend. When we stopped to speak, she exuded self-control. For the first time, it seemed like she was taking charge of her life. Since then, she's also found a new partner who values her, something her ex-husband didn't do, and she's become happier.[71]

The science of love and heartbreak
When you're in love, your body produces chemicals that make you feel good, such as dopamine – the reward hormone that makes

you feel giddy and euphoric – and norepinephrine – chemicals that make you feel alert and energetic.[73-75] When you're newly in love, the level of serotonin, a neurotransmitter that regulates mood, tends to be lower than in people who aren't in love.[76] Interestingly, diminished levels of serotonin are also seen in obsessive compulsive disorder. This may suggest why love can make you feel like you can't stop obsessing about the other person, and feelings of jealousy or anxiety arise.[77]

When you experience rejection, the same areas of the brain are stimulated as those implicated in drug addiction and craving, according to research by Stony Brook University, New York.[78] So being head-over-heels for someone who rejects you can often feel like a dependency – you crave the other person and can't stop thinking about them.

When you break up, the flood of feel-good chemicals such as dopamine (typical of a brain in love) ceases and your brain goes into 'withdrawal'.[79] Breakups sink our moods. For this reason, we need to turn to things that lift our moods again, give us pleasure and a sense of purpose.

HOW TO COPE: 5 STRATEGIES TO PROCESS HEARTBREAK

Reading time: 10 minutes

Here are five strategies we can use to bounce back from heartbreak and get that sense of purpose back.

1. The '3 benefits' exercise
Often, what can spur on growth after a breakup is to think of three ways that you benefited from the situation or from having been

with that person. Maybe now, for example, you have a better idea of the qualities you'd like to have in a future partner or you learned how to handle yourself better in future relationships. Even if it seems silly to do the '3 benefits' exercise, because all you might want to do is cry, give it a try. When we search for the positives and think of the things we might have gained in a painful situation, our mental health and wellbeing tend to fare better.[80] When people go through a breakup and try to find the meaning in it, this helps them bounce back. Sometimes a breakup is the motor we need to clarify our priorities and get onto the path that leads us closer to a more meaningful life. The '3 benefits' exercise can also help you foster positive emotions. So write down three positive aspects and then say them loudly to yourself – make sure you do this in a place in which you feel free to search within yourself and express your deepest thoughts (i.e. a private room).[72]

2. Develop the qualities you want in a partner

A breakup can be the catalyst we need to start reflecting on what we'd like in life, and especially what we'd like in our next partner. It can help us understand ourselves better.

Jenny, who had just been on the receiving end of a breakup, wrote to me about this:

'I've had an epiphany lately. I realized that basically this whole time, I couldn't attract the right kind of guy because I wasn't the right kind of girl, yet. In past years, I would wonder why guys didn't like me, I'd ask myself, "what's wrong with me?" or see them as jerks. But I realized that the qualities I wanted in a guy were often the things I didn't have. So I liked Mark because he had structure in his life (something I lacked), I liked Thomas because he was passionate about his work and had interests outside of work (things I was missing). You want in a guy what you want in yourself because you don't have it yet or are missing it. But I think if you start moulding yourself into the type of person that you'd like to meet and be with, you become happy.

When you become happy, it's easier to attract people and a partner that eventually shows love to you. You always hear these stories of people who hit rock bottom and then remake their lives: they stop smoking, get a job, became active, and eventually end up finding love. You never hear of someone who hits rock bottom, becomes an alcoholic and then finds love. This doesn't happen. So I believe that when you truly find yourself and meaning in your life, you find love too.'

3. Accept the fleetingness of relationships

If something makes us happy, we try to hold on to it and we don't want to let it go – and this can bring us suffering. But everything is always changing. This is why we can't hold on to things, even if they make us happy at one moment in time. The times that we had with people from our past might've been great but we can't wish for the good things we had to come back. We are meant to enjoy the love, the good things when they come to us, and then release them when it's their time to go. Use the experience as something that can shape you and move forward. When we let go, we can then move on to experience something else.

4. Meet with friends

When you're at your lowest, a good tip is to try to meet with (or call) friends. Being part of social networks buffers the impact of stress on our mental health. A study at Harvard showed that people who had strong relationships tended to feel happy in life.[83] While meeting up with your friends won't get rid of your heartbreak, it can make you feel better.

5. Use mercy as a powerful strategy

The last point that I would like to touch on is mercy. It's not something that books usually include and it's not something social media focuses on. But it's important. Mercy is the olive branch you extend to another person after they've wronged you. Even though you have every right to punish them, you *choose* to let it go. Maybe the other person is vulnerable in some way now, and instead of kicking them when they're down for past wrongs, you forgive.

When you develop a merciful attitude and forgive people, you start to feel more in control. If someone makes an error and you choose to let it go, you start to feel as if your errors can be forgiven too. You become less hard on yourself in those moments when you think you screwed up. And when it comes to relationships, this can give you closure.

Many times, we've heard the advice that it's good to get 'closure' after a relationship ends so that we can move on. And usually this means talking with the other person about why the relationship ended or asking them how you could've made things better. But doing this can be awkward. And even if you come face to face with your ex, they might not even provide you with the answers you're looking for. Getting closure doesn't necessarily have to involve interacting with the other person. It's something that can happen on your own, when you're alone in your home and it's just you and your thoughts. Getting closure can mean acknowl-

If you focus on the positive things in life,
you start to develop positive emotions.

edging to yourself that the other person has hurt you, but you've decided to forgive them anyway.

A monk I met during my travels said, 'you can forgive, but this does not mean that you should forget.' We don't forget, because we take the lessons we learned from the past into the future and these help shape us. We forgive because this gives us a sense of peace.

Bringing it all together

Breakups and divorces are hard to get through, but the way you see them, the way you cope with the pain, can help you bounce back. When you start focusing on what you've learned from the breakup and why it was good that it happened – even if it sounds silly to do so – this can help you change how you see the future. It can give you a new frame of reference. When you do things that are wholesome instead of things that are self-destructive, or when you develop a merciful attitude, that's when you can begin to move past what has happened. And see a spark of light in the darkness.

THINKING POSITIVE

Positive emotion is important for a number of reasons. We often think that feeling good has no consequence for us other than putting us in a good mood. But this is only a fraction of what happens. When you actively search for, and experience, positive emotions such as joy, you start to sharpen your skills. When you engage in situations which pique your interest, such as reading a new book or exploring a new hiking trail, this makes you feel a sense of possibility – and can be just the thing you need after a breakup or divorce. When you are open to new experiences, not only do you develop positive emotions, but you can counteract the bad moods.[81, 82]

Boosting the amount of positive emotion within you is a great antidote to negative feelings.[82] Positive moods have an *undoing effect*. If we feel bad and watch something that makes us feel cheerful, we recover quicker from bad feelings. Positive emotion helps build your inner resources. It helps you become tougher and you're better prepared to handle the next challenges that come your way. Here's an example: One study showed that people who watched a film that scared them recovered quicker from the fear if they then watched something that induced feelings of contentment or amusement in them. But other people who watched the fear-inducing film and then followed this up with something that only elicited *neutral* feelings in them took longer to let go of their fear.[82] So, as this simple example shows, when you look for ways to experience positive emotion, this can undo the effect of a bad mood. And it can have significant benefits for your wellbeing.

CHAPTER 9:

FEELING LOW?
How to find a sense of personal growth

I really hope this chapter helps you if you're looking for help right now. If you're struggling with a devastating financial situation, a terrible loss, or a serious illness, for example, then you're the person I've had in mind as I was writing this chapter.

When we're going through tough times, this can give way to overwhelm. Sometimes things happen that are beyond ourselves, beyond our powers of control, like the pandemic. I was asked by a magazine to write a piece on post-traumatic growth in light of the effect that the pandemic has had on our wellbeing. I'd like to share with you key things I discovered in my quest for the answers.

The first part of the chapter gives you a science-based tip to use in case of emergency: an immediate exercise to help you cope with a crisis. The rest of the chapter shows how tough times build stronger internal scaffolding within you and how they give you a new understanding of life – the evidence for this comes from hundreds of studies around the world. The last part of the chapter offers five long-term strategies to use during your most difficult life situations.

READ IN CASE OF EMERGENCY

- **Reframe your setback.** As silly as it may sound, think of three benefits of having experienced your setback. When you think of the benefits a situation can bring you, you often start to see things differently and begin to feel like you can cope. For example, a serious setback could put you on a different life path; a change in job is a chance to relocate or travel. Maybe now you enjoy the little things in life more (e.g. family dinners) that you might've taken for granted before.

THE SCIENCE OF POST-TRAUMATIC GROWTH

Reading time: 🕐 10 minutes

When you lose someone or something important to you, or receive terrible news, you tend to hear about how bad it is, how tough times and challenges can make you depressed and spiral down-wards. And while all this can happen and it is indeed devastating, you have to know that going through something difficult can make you tougher. Stronger. Going through something distressing can build internal scaffolding that can help you weather even tougher storms in the future.[73] This phenomenon is called 'post-traumatic growth'.

When we're going through life, we all have beliefs and concep-tions about the world that ground us. That make us feel safe and secure so that we can focus on what we're doing in the present moment and let go of the rest. These conceptions give us a sense of stability. For example, we might assume that life is predictable – we think that if we work hard, our boss will be happy and we'll get a promotion, or if we take good care of our health now, we won't get sick later. But when disaster strikes – you find out you have a disease or you lose your job even though you've worked hard – your beliefs can shatter. Your beliefs have been violated, are no longer valid, and if you want to retain your mental equilibrium, you have to take a second look at them. You may have to take a closer look at your assumptions and maybe even replace them.[84]

Tough times can change you

There's no denying that tough times are hard to go through. They can make you feel hopeless and even depressed. When my mother was diagnosed with cancer a second time, I felt like my world was changing. I felt numb and didn't understand why this was happening to her. She always led such a healthy and active life and was too young to have this happen to her: she was only 58. I found it difficult to cope and sadness would overtake me, sometimes out of the blue: I'd suddenly feel this sinking sensation in my stomach and I couldn't see clearly anymore. Sometimes it would happen at the most inopportune of times: while at work, on the crowded bus, on my way home from work, while talking to someone who looked carefree.

But somehow the harder the struggle become, the more I noticed that things within me were starting to change; it was almost like I was holding out an invisible hand to other people so I could grab on to them for help. I started feeling a closer bond to the world. I remember one day after work, a young woman was handing out leaflets in the city centre and usually, I would never take these because I had no use for them. My mother always would though, whenever someone passed them out to her, and when I asked her why, she would say it was 'the kind thing to do.' For years, I couldn't fully understand how that would make any difference, but in that moment, when I was going through one of the darkest moments of my life, I got it. In that moment, someone was extending their arm out to me. Granted, she was only holding a leaflet and she was doing this to everyone passing by. But I felt like, in that moment, I could make this person's day a little brighter and could accept the leaflet instead of refusing it. And so, I took it. I smiled at her and thanked her and she smiled back. And that brief interaction, that friendly glance she gave me for my small gesture boosted my mood and, that afternoon, I didn't feel so alone anymore. This deepening of bonds and appreciating the little things is exactly what is happening during post-traumatic growth.[84]

When my mother had her first breast cancer, her test results were lost by her family doctor for months, delaying her treatment. This might have had a negative impact on her prognosis. The diagnosis and rumination over the lost test results traumatized her.

But after she finished treatment, my mother told me that the whole experience changed her: she began feeling more connected to nature and wanted to start travelling. She stopped thinking about what had happened and only began to look forward in life. After the cancer returned as a metastasis several years later, she changed even more. After a few months of intense struggling and coming to terms with the new reality, my mother realized that the present is the most important moment. Ironically, getting sick a second time made her fear *less*, not more, and she started understanding life in a new way. She was neither clinging to life in a desperate attempt to prolong it nor struggling. Instead, she decided to enjoy each day.

When we're experiencing post-traumatic growth, all sorts of unanticipated changes can happen. You can start to see life in a new way. Often people who have survived great distress say that they have developed a new appreciation for life. They might have even found a new purpose, 'the call of a potential meaning waiting to be fulfilled' as the neurologist Viktor Frankl would say. And this purpose can be as simple and yet as profound as realizing that the monotonous job you have isn't bringing you any happiness and you need a change. One woman who had been diagnosed with cancer realized that she wasn't enjoying her career and decided to become a nurse to cancer patients, because this brought her meaning.[04, 85]

Post-traumatic growth can help you grow in unanticipated ways. It can help you grow spiritually and make you realize that you're stronger than you might've thought. Judith Viorst wrote about loss and trauma, and in her book[86] she quotes counsellor Rabbi Harold Kushner, whose son had passed away. Rabbi Kushner thought back to this tragic incident when he said:[84, 86]

'I am a more sensitive person , a more effective pastor, a more sympathetic counsellor because of Aaron's life and death than I would ever have been without it. And I would give up all of those gains in a second if I could have my son back. If I could choose, I

would forego all of the spiritual growth and depth which has come my way because of our experiences … But I cannot choose.'

What is interesting is that when we experience hardship and we surpass it, we often don't just go back to the way we were. We become a stronger version of our previous self. And the changes are often positive in the longrun. If you're going through a tough time and are looking for ways to encourage this post-traumatic growth process or achieve mental wellbeing, there are a few things you can do:

HOW TO COPE: 5 STRATEGIES FOR BOUNCING BACK

Reading time: 🕐 10 minutes

1. Don't suppress your emotions

Ichiro Kawachi, a researcher at Harvard, showed that trying to escape or block out what you're feeling can increase the risk for premature mortality.[87] Because you're not releasing the pent-up anger, frustration or sadness, this may affect your health and lead to potentially harmful forms of coping with these feelings – such as over-eating or drinking.[87,88]

When people suppress their emotions, they also tend to feel less satisfied with their life and their self-esteem suffers. Keeping emotions bottled up can make people feel inauthentic – they may be trying to maintain an outward appearance of calm or control while on the inside, they're well-aware they're struggling. This discrepancy between how they look – the mask they're putting on to the outside world – and how they really feel can further sink their moods.[89]

So if you're going through something difficult and feel sad, angry or frustrated, instead of suppressing uncomfortable emotions, allow them to course through your body. Don't try to numb yourself out, instead feel the feelings.

2. Put it down on paper

One thing that we can do to facilitate the healing process is to write it down. Research shows that when we're going through a trauma and we write about it, we begin to feel better mentally and physically. The tension starts to go down and we begin functioning better. But the *way* you write about it is important. In a study[90] on coping with trauma and stress, some participants were told to write only about their emotions surrounding the event, while others were told to write about not only their emotions – but importantly *how they made sense of the situation*. Turns out that those who wrote about their thoughts, feelings and how they made sense of the situation experienced increases in positive growth from trauma while the others didn't. The results of this study are both unexpected and fascinating. When you do the writing exercise, it can help you and set you on the path to move forward.

Why is self-disclosure so helpful? When we open up about what we went through, when we write about it, we can resolve 'unresolved issues'. When something happens that upsets us deeply, we can feel momentarily off balance and the internal scaffolding that we've got might be too weak to support us.

When we don't express or articulate our thoughts, they can confuse us because they're vague and lack any kind of shape. But have you ever noticed that as soon as you begin to disclose about a problem – even if it's just by writing about it – you start to see things more clearly and you might even get an idea for how to handle it? When we're trying to articulate what we're feeling, we're making the emotion that's coursing through our body concrete. When we take a thought and we put it down on paper, it's not vague anymore: we give it shape and it's specific. And in the process, we gain clarity. Regardless of whether you share your thoughts with others or keep them to yourself, the benefits you will experience are great.

3. Talk about it with people who have been through it too

When we go through tough times, we might also choose to talk to other people who've been through the same thing. This is also important for encouraging the post-traumatic growth process. Research shows that when you share your experience with others, such as those in a support group[84] who went through the same thing as you, you often learn how these people handled similar situations. You learn about different perspectives, you learn about different beliefs and you may choose to adopt these beliefs in order to build stronger internal scaffolding for yourself. Scaffolding that not only better supports you against future shocks, but also helps you see how this event fits within the larger context of life. Scaffolding that gives *meaning* to your suffering.

4. Try physical activity

When you do physical activity, endorphins are released in your body. Endorphins diminish the perception of pain and can act as sedatives, which can help you when you're going through difficulties.[91] Scientists say that exercise 'acts as a drug' – it can even become addictive.[91] So take up light jogging or any other physical activity and the regular flow of endorphins will help you start feeling better over time. In studies, physical activity has been shown to help with depression and anxiety and can reduce premature mortality, among a host of other health benefits.[92, 93]

5. Consider religion or spirituality

Albert Einstein is one of the greatest scientists that's ever lived; a man who changed the way we think about gravity, heavily influenced modern physics, and received the Nobel Prize for his work. It was also Albert Einstein who said: 'the more I study science, the more I believe in God'. The next chapter will show you how religion and spirituality may answer some of life's most difficult questions and help you in situations in which you find it hard to cope. It will show you how, for some, turning to a higher power can be a catalyst to wisdom and strength.

Bringing it all together

Going through a tough time is difficult. It can lead to feelings of depression, anger and despair. But while it's hard to experience these emotions, tough times also have a strengthening effect and can help you find a sense of personal growth. Knowing this can take away some of the fear – the fear about more tough times coming your way over the years.

Life is unpredictable. But one thing is for sure: people are often stronger than they realize and when we hold on and don't give up hope, we often find a way to make it through to the other end. As an old saying goes: 'Our greatest glory is not in never falling, but in rising every time we fall.'

By putting things down on paper, we learn more about ourselves.

CHAPTER 10:

FEELING LET DOWN?
How to find hope

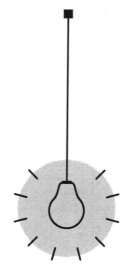

The modernization of society has made us more secular and we've been increasingly relying on science for the answers. But sometimes, people still have an innate need to bring meaning into their lives and look for answers beyond the science. Answers that can be found through a different dimension: a sacred sphere that surpasses material or physical things and that can provide a sense of peace.

This chapter looks at why people turn to religion in times of greatest need, and how different types of prayer can affect your mental health and wellbeing. We will also look at spirituality and why people have turned to it to find wisdom and guidance. Practices like meditation and yoga are popular all over the globe, and millions have flocked to reiki gurus and spiritual teachers, to find hope.

If you'd like to tap into the sacred sphere and would like some quick tips on hand, try one of the 'Read in case of emergency' ideas, below:

READ IN CASE OF EMERGENCY

- **Collect leaves and rocks.** One thing you can do to tap into spirituality is go outside and immerse yourself in nature. Pick up a few leaves and rocks that you like. This tip may sound simple, but doing this can have a soothing effect when you're going through a crisis. In that brief moment when you're touching a leaf and hearing its crackle in your hand, or feeling the smooth texture of the rock, you might feel a sense of relief from this material world: the pure, natural leaf contrasted with the plastic we touch on a daily basis, everything that's artificial created by humankind. And you get back to basics.

- **Consider praying with a friend.** This creates a sense of bonding and being listened to. You are opening yourself up to God and your friend is by your side. A feeling of support is created.

THE PSYCHOLOGY OF PRAYER

Reading time: 🕐 10 minutes

When we're going through our most difficult moments in life, and our moods are at their lowest, this is when we are at our most vulnerable. These are often the times when our tried-and-tested methods of coping might no longer be working for us, and we are looking for new ways to make it through. This is also the time when we are most susceptible to adopting a new belief system. And in our search for help, we might turn to religion.

Religion can be more than just going to a place of worship or reading texts on a regular basis, as some may think. Religion can be something you engage in on your own when you're alone in your room asking for help, any help that can get you through difficult times. It may be the last remnant of hope that you cling to when everything else has failed. It can also be something that you deeply hold within yourself as you go about your day-to-day life.

The way you use religion can have a profound impact on your mental health. Your religious beliefs can either increase your sense of wellbeing and inner peace, or can lead you to a state of anxiety and depression. Therefore, we have to take a closer look at what this concept is and the different ways of coping within this context.

What is religion?
Religion has to do with the sacred. It's a dimension that people turn to when they want answers to questions that are unanswerable. Questions like: 'what is the point of life?' and 'what happens

to us after we die?' If you're suffering, you might be trying to understand why you're experiencing whatever you're going through, if there is any meaning behind it. When we see a point to the difficulties we endure, they can become a little easier to bear.[94]

Religion can provide people with comfort and a sense of control, and many of us turn to religion to cope at critical times such as job loss, illness, divorce or financial problems. It can be a source of support when there's no one else to turn to.

I remember, many years ago, seeing a picture of golden sand in a desert and a trail of footprints in the sand. Next to the image, the text read something like: 'Father, in my darkest moments, you deserted me. I was in pain and needed you the most, but in those moments, you were nowhere to be found. I was praying for you to help me, you should've been walking by my side, but I can only see my footprints.' And to this, God answered: 'My son, in your darkest, toughest moments, I was carrying you. When you couldn't go on anymore, I picked you up. When your strength left you, I took you in my arms. This is why there is only one set of footsteps.' The meaning of this has stayed with me all these years and, for me, exemplifies the essence of religion.

Religion and self-esteem

Religion doesn't just provide us with a sense of comfort, but can also help shape our self-esteem. People who see their body as something sacred are more likely to take care of it, to nourish it and avoid excesses. When you see your body as something sacred, you may value yourself a little more. This isn't to say that being religious means that you will take good care of yourself; it just means that people who view their bodies as valuable[94, 95] might be more likely to take better care of themselves.

What praying can teach us

Everyone's way of praying is different. If you're a believer or you practise religion, how you engage in this can also affect your wellbeing. Let's take a look at two praying styles and see how these can affect us and how we see ourselves:

The collaborative approach

One method of relating to God is the 'collaborative approach'.[96] People who go by this approach tackle their problems with God as a partner by their side. They work together with God to solve the issues they've got. These people take an active problem-solving stance. Active problem-solving has been linked to improved mental wellbeing.

The deferral approach

Others use a 'deferral approach' when they pray.[96] They defer or pass their problems on to God and pray that they get solved. This approach is used more often by people who might not feel as competent in their lives and see God as a deity that provides them with all the answers. They tend to shy away from trying to find solutions themselves and can be fearful to experiment with life. A deferral approach might limit you: for example, if you've fallen behind in your work, praying to God will not do much if you're not taking any steps yourself to improve the situation, you need to start reading the papers or writing the report. In this case, deferring your stress and problems to God takes away from your sense of responsibility. And it takes away from what *you* can do to change your situation. This is why the old sailor's proverb 'I'm going to pray to God, but continue rowing to shore' might be good guidance to go by.

In other instances, deferring can be a tremendously helpful approach. For example, if you're dealing with circumstances that are beyond your control, such as a serious illness or accident.[96] Using this praying style can take a load off your mind to know that even though there's nothing else you can do, you can rely on a higher power. According to research, people with advanced cancer who were religious and turned to prayer in some of their toughest moments experienced less pain than others.[97]

Praying can be an active approach to life

Some people might think that prayer is a passive approach to life's problems. But research shows that this isn't necessarily true: there is rich diversity when it comes to religious coping.[98] If you're engaging in a 'collaborative approach', for example, you are trying to solve your problem and are taking responsibility. You're not a passive recipient; you're taking action.

Our beliefs about God have an impact

Another important aspect when it comes to religion is the way you view God. Is your overall perception of God as a loving, supportive figure or a presence that can punish and harm you? This can have a significant impact on your wellbeing.

In research studies, people who trusted that God was by their side fared better when it came to their mental health. People who nurtured a positive relationship with God, and saw this as a force for good, had less stress and higher levels of positive mood than others.[98]

On the other hand, people who believed that their misfortunes were punishment from God for their sins or who felt let down didn't fare as well. People who believed that God had limited power and couldn't bring about the things they prayed for also tended to spiral downwards. Anytime there was tension and struggle in their relationship with God, this was linked to anxiety and depression.[98-100] One woman I met wasn't feeling well and started praying for God's help. After months of praying, the illness was still there, and so she started thinking that God had limited abilities to help her or maybe had forgotten about her. This negative perception not only plummeted her mood, but it added to the distress she was already feeling.

Any time there's struggle or conflict when we're thinking about God, this can negatively affect our mental health. But when we view God only as just and loving, this is better for our mental health. We fare better, because we've found a sense of peace.

The presence of religion in your life can vary. Maybe God is not at the centre of your life, but is just one member in your support network that you can draw on whenever you need spiritual or emotional help. We can have a support network made up of various people: family, friends and co-workers; and we go to different members of this network for different needs. According to research, God can be one of these members.[101, 102]

Here is a message I received from Christoph, who wrote to me about how God and developing 'belief' helped him:

'God can't work for you or do your work, but every once in a while, you suddenly get a small idea pop in your head about what course of action to take and you almost feel like "maybe I should try it". Or maybe you get an idea about someone to talk to that could help you out with a problem. And then you try it. And you have a little bit more hope than all the other times that it's going to work out. You feel more optimistic.'

SPIRITUALITY

Some people don't identify with religion and God, but, instead, turn to spirituality in their quest for answers. They turn to spiritual practices such as mindfulness, yoga and meditation to bring meaning into their lives. It's not mutually exclusive though: you can pray to God while also engaging in spirituality. You might not see these practices as 'spiritual', but you can still experience the benefits. Here are five strategies on how you can develop spirituality:

HOW TO COPE: 5 STRATEGIES FOR EXPLORING YOUR SPIRITUALITY

Reading time: ⏱ 10 minutes

1. Listen to uplifting music

When we listen to something uplifting, it often triggers a sense of something more in us – a yearning to find *meaning*. Music can make us feel good and spiritually-enriched. According to science, listening to music has a whole host of benefits: it lowers anxiety, decreases pain and may even have positive effects on the brain.[103] A study showed that listening to Mozart for 10 minutes can have a positive effect on people's spatial temporal reasoning (spatial awareness)[104] – this has been dubbed the 'Mozart effect'. Even rats who listen to Mozart seem to do better in mazes: they're quicker and make fewer mistakes compared to rats who listen to white noise, silence or minimalist music.[105] It seems that listening to uplifting music has a positive effect on our minds and could be something we turn to in moments of need.

2. Travelling

Travelling to new places can stimulate thoughts, reflections and musings. Seeing a new landscape and breathing in the fresh air in a new city can be invigorating and help us feel spiritually enriched. Travelling can help you understand what you want out of life and realize what you should be letting go of – the little things that are unimportant but that disturb our mental equilibrium far too often. If you can't go far, even a day trip can change things up.

3. The causes of suffering

According to Buddhist monks, our minds are often the sources of our unhappiness. So if unhappiness arises in the mind, then it follows that the causes of happiness and suffering are also in the mind. Sometimes we rationalize things too much, looking for evidence and a clear, definable path towards belief – but by its very nature, the spiritual dimension is difficult to measure. If we see something helps us and we go back to it – this is all the evidence

> People who believe that God let them down or punished them for their sins tend to have poorer wellbeing than those who believe God is there to help them.

we need. For example, if you find a moment of peace in meditation, it is telling you that this works for you. Whenever something upsetting happens, always go back to that moment.

4. Recognize that happiness is peace of mind

We often equate happiness with excitement: we think that if we get that new iPhone, see an amazing band, get that text message we've been craving, we'll be happy. It's true that once we get these things, we do feel a boost in positive emotions, but our excitement wears off quickly. We're back to where we started and still not feeling as happy as we'd like.

Mindfulness meditation shows that happiness is something less complicated, it's much more subtle, it doesn't rely on material items. Happiness comes from having peace of mind. The more you cultivate moments that can bring calmness and serenity in your life, the happier you start to feel.

5. Walk barefoot on grass

Something else that can help you tap into spirituality is walking barefoot on grass, also known as 'grounding' or 'earthing'. When you walk through the grass barefoot, this offers a sensation unlike any other. It almost forces you to pay attention to the present moment, the bumps and soft earth below the sole of your foot, the unexpected pricks, the sense of happiness you get. When you walk barefoot on the earth, you start to feel a connection with nature, a feeling of being grounded, a feeling of spirituality.

Bringing it all together

Some people turn to spirituality and some people turn to religion whenever they need help or want to find a deeper meaning. Others use both. Even if you feel you don't have a belief system and would like to explore this more, you can take it step by step: join a mindfulness meditation class or read about how religion can help you.

Many people around the globe turn to a higher power for help because, sometimes the going gets tough. This is why, when we take someone's hand to hold every so often and *believe* – whether it's in religion or spirituality or whatever you name it – this can make our falls a little easier to bear. And our getting up becomes possible.

Listening to music lowers anxiety and decreases pain.

AFTERWORD

I'd like to close this book with a thought. People have written to me over the years telling me they are struggling with moods and wanted to know what they can do: the man who was paralyzed by indecision, the student who procrastinated, the woman who couldn't stop worrying about a mistake she'd made. People like these were the ones I've had in the back of my mind as I was writing this book. To show that there is another way. A way that allows you to bounce back no matter what mood you're in and become the person you want to be. At any age, no matter where you're at in life and the hand you've been dealt. I hope you find this book helpful and that through it, you find a way forward that works for you.

REFERENCES

1. Dijksterhuis, A., et al., *On making the right choice: the deliberation-without-attention effect.* Science, 2006. **311**(5763): p. 1005–7.

2. Douglas, K. and D. Jones, *Top 10 ways to make better decisions*, in *New Scientist* 2007, https://www.newscientist.com/article/mg19426021-100-top-10-ways-to-make-better-decisions/.

3. Schwartz, B., et al., *Maximizing versus satisficing: happiness is a matter of choice.* J Pers Soc Psychol, 2002. **83**(5): p. 1178–97.

4. Iyengar, S.S. and M.R. Lepper, *When choice is demotivating: can one desire too much of a good thing?* J Pers Soc Psychol, 2000. **79**(6): p. 995–1006.

5. Wilson, T. and D. Gilbert, *Affective Forecasting: Knowing What to Want.* Curr Dir Psychol Science, 2005. **14**(3): p. 131–34.

6. Gilbert, D.T., et al., *Immune neglect: a source of durability bias in affective forecasting.* J Pers Soc Psychol, 1998. **75**(3): p. 617–38.

7. Carpenter, S. *We don't know our own strength*, in *American Psychological Association*, 2001, https://www.apa.org/monitor/oct01/strength.

8. Marchetti, I., et al., *Self-generated thoughts and depression: from daydreaming to depressive symptoms.* Front Hum Neurosci, 2014. **8**(131): p. 1–10.

9. Marchetti, I., et al., *Spontaneous Thought and Vulnerability to Mood Disorders: The Dark Side of the Wandering Mind.* Clin Psychol Sci, 2016. **4**(5): p. 835–857.

10. Tice, D.M. and R.F. Baumeister, *Longitudinal study of procrastination, performance, stress, and health: the costs and benefits of dawdling.* Psychol Sci, 1997. **8**(6): p. 454–58.

11. Svartdal, F., et al., *On the Behavioral Side of Procrastination: Exploring Behavioral Delay in Real-Life Settings.* Front Psychol, 2018. **9**: p. 746.

12. Hajloo, N., *Relationships between self-efficacy, self-esteem and procrastination in undergraduate psychology students.* Iran J Psychiatry Behav Sci, 2014. **8**(3): p. 42–9.

13. Gallwey, W.T., *The Inner Game of Work: Focus, Learning, Pleasure, and Mobility in the Workplace.* 2001: Random House Publishing Group.

14. Pychyl, T.A., *Solving the Procrastination Puzzle: A Concise Guide to Strategies for Change.* 2013: Jeremy P. Tarcher/Penguin, a member of Penguin Group (USA).

15. Gilbert, D.T. and T.D. Wilson, *Why the brain talks to itself: sources of error in emotional prediction.* Philos Trans R Soc Lond B Biol Sci, 2009. **364**(1521): p. 1335-41.

16. Eldufani, J., et al., *Nonanesthetic Effects of Ketamine: A Review Article.* Am J Med, 2018. **131**(12): p. 1418-1424.

17. Dweck, C., *Mindset - Updated Edition: Changing The Way You think To Fulfil Your Potential.* 2017: Little, Brown Book Group.

18. Haase, C.M., et al., *Happiness as a motivator: positive affect predicts primary control striving for career and educational goals.* Pers Soc Psychol Bull, 2012. **38**(8): p. 1093-104.

19. Baumeister, R., et al., *Losing Control: How and Why People Fail at Self-Regulation.* 1994: Elsevier Science.

20. Mischel, W., et al., *The nature of adolescent competencies predicted by preschool delay of gratification.* J Pers Soc Psychol, 1988. **54**(4): p. 687-96.

21. Moffitt, T.E., et al., *A gradient of childhood self-control predicts health, wealth, and public safety.* Proc Natl Acad Sci USA, 2011. **108**(7): p. 2693-8.

22. Stromback, C., et al., *Does self-control predict financial behavior and financial well-being?* J Behav Exp Finance, 2017. **14**: p. 30-38.

23. Duckworth, A.L., et al., *What No Child Left Behind Leaves Behind: The Roles of IQ and Self-Control in Predicting Standardized Achievement Test Scores and Report Card Grades.* J Educ Psychol, 2012. **104**(2): p. 439-451.

24. Sternberg, R.J., *Intelligence.* Dialogues Clin Neurosci, 2012. **14**(1): p. 19-27.

25. Wong, M.M. and M. Csikszentmihalyi, *Motivation and academic achievement: the effects of personality traits and the quality of experience.* J Pers, 1991. **59**(3): p. 539-74.

26. Remes, O., et al., *A strong sense of coherence associated with reduced risk of anxiety disorder among women in disadvantaged circumstances: British population study.* BMJ Open, 2018. **8**(4): p. e018501.

27. Park, N., et al., *Character strengths in fifty-four nations and the fifty US states.* J Posit Psychol, 2007. **1**(3): p. 118-29.

28. Muraven, M. and R.F. Baumeister, *Self-regulation and depletion of limited resources: does self-control resemble a muscle?* Psychol Bull, 2000. **126**(2): p. 247-59.

29. Baumeister, R.F., et al., *Ego depletion: is the active self a limited resource?* J Pers Soc Psychol, 1998. **74**(5): p. 1252-65.

30. Muraven, M. and D. Shmueli, *The self-control costs of fighting the temptation to drink.* Psychol Addict Behav, 2006. **20**(2): p. 154-60.

31. Duckworth, A.L., et al., *Situational Strategies for Self-Control*. Perspect Psychol Sci, 2016. **11**(1): p. 35–55.

32. Muraven, M., et al., *Longitudinal improvement of self-regulation through practice: building self-control strength through repeated exercise*. J Soc Psychol, 1999. **139**(4): p. 446–57.

33. Tice, D.M., et al., *Restoring the self: Positive affect helps improve self-regulation following ego depletion*. J Exp Soc Psychol 2007. **43**: p. 379–84.

34. Fowler, J.H. and N.A. Christakis, *Dynamic spread of happiness in a large social network: longitudinal analysis over 20 years in the Framingham Heart Study*. BMJ, 2008. **337**: p. a2338.

35. McGhee, P., *Humor as Survival Training for a Stressed-Out World: The 7 Humor Habits Program*. 2010: AuthorHouse.

36. Marziali, E., et al., *The role of coping humor in the physical and mental health of older adults*. Aging Ment Health, 2008. **12**(6): p. 713–8.

37. Samson, A.C. and J.J. Gross, *Humour as emotion regulation: the differential consequences of negative versus positive humour*. Cogn Emot, 2012. **26**(2): p. 375–84.

38. Ford, T.E., et al., *Effect of humor on state anxiety and math performance*. Humor, 2012. **25**(1): p. 59–74.

39. Daviu, N., et al., *Neurobiological links between stress and anxiety*. Neurobiol Stress, 2019. **11**: p. 100191.

40. Fredrickson, B.L. and T. Joiner, *Positive emotions trigger upward spirals toward emotional well-being*. Psychol Sci, 2002. **13**(2): p. 172–5.

41. Fredrickson, B.L., *The broaden-and-build theory of positive emotions*. Philos Trans R Soc Lond B Biol Sci, 2004. **359**(1449): p. 1367–78.

42. Tagalidou, N., et al., *Feasibility of a Humor Training to Promote Humor and Decrease Stress in a Subclinical Sample: A Single-Arm Pilot Study*. Front Psychol, 2018. **9**: p. 577.

43. Henman, L., *Humor, control & human connection: lessons from the Vietnam POWs*. Humor, 2001. 14(1): p.83–94.

44. McGhee, P. *Using Humor to cope; humor in concentration/POW camps*. https://www.laughterremedy.com/article_pdfs/Using%20Humor%20 to%20Cope-Part%202.pdf.

45. Uvnäs-Moberg, K., et al., *Self-soothing behaviors with particular reference to oxytocin release induced by non-noxious sensory stimulation*. Front Psychol, 2014. **5**: p. 1529.

46. Simpson, H.B., et al., *Anxiety Disorders: Theory, Research and Clinical Perspectives*. 2010: Cambridge University Press.

47. Hecht, D., *The neural basis of optimism and pessimism*. Exp Neurobiol, 2013. **22**(3): p. 173–99.

48. Carver, C.S., et al., *Optimism*. Clin Psychol Rev, 2010. **30**(7): p. 879–89.

49. Ironson, G., et al., *Dispositional optimism and the mechanisms by which it predicts slower disease progression in HIV: proactive behavior, avoidant coping, and depression*. Int J Behav Med, 2005. **12**(2): p. 86–97.

50. Ramírez-Maestre, C., R. et al., *The role of optimism and pessimism in chronic pain patients adjustment*. Span J Psychol, 2012. **15**(1): p. 286–94.

51. Jacobson, N.S., et al., *Behavioral activation treatment for depression: returning to contextual roots*. Clin Psychol Sci Prac, 2001. **8**: p. 15.

52. Jacobson, N.S. and E.T. Gortner, *Can depression be de-medicalized in the 21st century: scientific revolutions, counter-revolutions and the magnetic field of normal science*. Behav Res Ther, 2000. **38**(2): p. 103–17.

53. Martell, C.R., et al., *Depression in Context: Strategies for Guided Action*. 2001: W.W. Norton.

54. NcNiel, J.M. and W. Fleeson, *The causal effects of extraversion on positive affect and neuroticism on negative affect: Manipulating state extraversion and state neuroticism in an experimental approach*. J Res Pers, 2006. **40**(5): p. 529–50.

55. British Red Cross. *Covid-19 and isolation: helpful things to remember about loneliness*, https://www.redcross.org.uk/stories/disasters-and-emergencies/uk/coronavirus-six-facts-about-loneliness.

56. Cacioppo, J.T. and S. Cacioppo, *The growing problem of loneliness*. Lancet, 2018. **391**(10119): p. 426.

57. Murthy, V. *Work and the Loneliness Epidemic*, in *Harvard Business Review*, 2017, https://hbr.org/2017/09/work-and-the-loneliness-epidemic.

58. Hawkley, L.C. and J.T. Cacioppo, *Loneliness matters: a theoretical and empirical review of consequences and mechanisms*. Ann Behav Med, 2010. **40**(2): p. 218–27.

59. Rico-Uribe, L.A., et al., *Association of loneliness with all-cause mortality: A meta-analysis*. PLoS One, 2018. **13**(1): p. e0190033.

60. Kiecolt-Glaser, J.K., et al., *Urinary cortisol levels, cellular immunocompetency, and loneliness in psychiatric inpatients*. Psychosom Med, 1984. **46**(1): p. 15–23.

61. Caspi, A., et al., *Socially isolated children 20 years later: risk of cardiovascular disease*. Arch Pediatr Adolesc Med, 2006. **160**(8): p. 805–11.

62. Epley, N. and J. Schroeder, *Mistakenly seeking solitude*. J Exp Psychol Gen, 2014. **143**(5): p. 1980–99.

63. Epley, N. and J. Schroeder, *The surprising benefits of talking to strangers*, in *BBC News*, 2019, https://www.bbc.co.uk/news/world-48459940.

64. Burridge, T., *Crossing Divides: Can a 'chatty bus' combat loneliness?*, in *BBC News*, 2019, https://www.bbc.co.uk/news/uk-48622007.

65. Spithoven, A.W.M., et al., *It is all in their mind: A review on information processing bias in lonely individuals.* Clin Psychol Rev, 2017. **58**: p. 97–114.

66. Baumeister, R.F., et al., *Social exclusion impairs self-regulation.* J Pers Soc Psychol, 2005. **88**(4): p. 589–604.

67. Newall, N.E., et al., *Causal beliefs, social participation, and loneliness among older adults: A longitudinal study.* J Soc Pers Relat, 2009. **26**(2): p. 273–90.

68. Sprecher, S., et al., *Factors Associated with Distress Following the Breakup of a Close Relationship.* J Soc Pers Relat 1998. **15**(6): p. 791–809.

69. Newman, H.M. and E.J. Langer, *Post-divorce adaptation and the attribution of responsibility.* Sex Roles, 1981. **7**: p. 223–32.

70. Tashiro, T. and P. Frazier, *"I'll never be in a relationship like that again": Personal growth following romantic relationship breakups.* Pers Relatsh, 2003. **10**(1): p. 113–128.

71. Kansky, J. and J.P. Allen, *Making Sense and Moving On: The Potential for Individual and Interpersonal Growth Following Emerging Adult Breakups.* Emerg Adulthood, 2018. **6**(3): p. 172–190.

72. Lewandowski, G.W., *Promoting positive emotions following relationship dissolution through writing.* J Posit Psychol, 2009. **4**(1): p. 21–31.

73. Aron, A., et al., *Reward, motivation, and emotion systems associated with early-stage intense romantic love.* J Neurophysiol, 2005. **94**(1): p. 327–37.

74. Seshadri, K.G., *The neuroendocrinology of love.* Indian J Endocrinol Metab, 2016. **20**(4): p. 558–63.

75. Wu, K., *Love, Actually: The science behind lust, attraction, and companionship*, in Harvard University, The Graduate School of Arts and Sciences, http://sitn.hms.harvard.edu/flash/2017/love-actually-science-behind-lust-attraction-companionship/.

76. Marazziti, D., et al., *Alteration of the platelet serotonin transporter in romantic love.* Psychol Med, 1999. **29**(3): p. 741–5.

77. Stromberg, J., *This is your brain on love*, in *Vox*, 2015, https://www.vox.com/2015/2/12/8025525/love-neuroscience.

78. Stony Brook University, *Anguish Of Romantic Rejection May Be Linked To Stimulation Of Areas Of Brain Related To Motivation, Reward And Addiction*, in *Science Daily*, 2010, https://www.sciencedaily.com/releases/2010/07/100722142201.htm.

79. Mark, C., *Broken heart, broken brain: The neurology of breaking up and how to get over it*, in *CBC*, 2018, https://www.cbc.ca/life/wellness/broken-heart-broken-brain-the-neurology-of-breaking-up-and-how-to-get-over-it-1.4608785.

80. Helgeson, V.S., et al., *A meta-analytic review of benefit finding and growth.* J Consult Clin Psychol, 2006. **74**(5): p. 797–816.

81. Fredrickson, B.L., *What Good Are Positive Emotions?* Rev Gen Psychol, 1998. **2**(3): p. 300–319.

82. Fredrickson, B.L. and R.W. Levenson, *Positive Emotions Speed Recovery from the Cardiovascular Sequelae of Negative Emotions.* Cogn Emot, 1998. **12**(2): p. 191–220.

83. Mineo, L. *Harvard study, almost 80 years old, has proved that embracing community helps us live longer, and be happier.* 2017, https://news.harvard.edu/gazette/story/2017/04/over-nearly-80-years-harvard-study-has-been-showing-how-to-live-a-healthy-and-happy-life/.

84. R Tedeschi, L.C., *Posttraumatic growth: conceptual foundations and empirical evidence.* Psychol Inq, 2004. **15**(1): p. 1–18.

85. Tedeschi, R.G., et al., *Posttraumatic Growth: Theory, Research, and Applications.* 2018: Taylor & Francis.

86. Viorst, J., *Necessary Losses.* 1986: Simon and Schuster.

87. Chapman, B.P., et al., *Emotion suppression and mortality risk over a 12-year follow-up.* J Psychosom Res, 2013. **75**(4): p. 381–5.

88. Nathan Consedine, C.M., et al., *Moderators of the Emotion Inhibition-Health Relationship: A Review and Research Agenda.* Rev Gen Psychol, 2002. **6**(2): p. 204–28.

89. Gross, J.J. and O.P. John, *Individual differences in two emotion regulation processes: implications for affect, relationships, and well-being.* J Pers Soc Psychol, 2003. **85**(2): p. 348–62.

90. Ullrich, P.M. and S.K. Lutgendorf, *Journaling about stressful events: effects of cognitive processing and emotional expression.* Ann Behav Med, 2002. **24**(3): p. 244–50.

91. Vina, J., et al., *Exercise acts as a drug; the pharmacological benefits of exercise.* Br J Pharmacol, 2012. **167**(1): p. 1–12.

92. Murri, M.B., et al., *Physical Exercise in Major Depression: Reducing the Mortality Gap While Improving Clinical Outcomes.* Front Psychiatry, 2018. **9**: p. 762.

93. Anderson, E. and G. Shivakumar, *Effects of exercise and physical activity on anxiety.* Front Psychiatry, 2013. **4**: p. 27.

94. Pargament, K.I., *The Psychology of Religion and Coping: Theory, Research, Practice.* 2001: Guilford Publications.

95. Pargament, K., et al., *The Brief RCOPE: Current Psychometric Status of a Short Measure of Religious Coping.* Religions, 2011. **2**: p. 51–76.

96. Pargament, K., et al., *Religion and the Problem-Solving Process: Three Styles of Coping.* J Sci Study Relig, 1988. **27**(1): p. 90.

97. Yates, J.W., et al., *Religion in patients with advanced cancer.* Med Pediatr Oncol, 1981. **9**(2): p. 121–8.

98. Pargament, K.I., et al., *The many methods of religious coping: development and initial validation of the RCOPE.* J Clin Psychol, 2000. **56**(4): p. 519–43.

99. O'Brien, B., et al., *Positive and negative religious coping as predictors of distress among minority older adults.* Int J Geriatr Psychiatry, 2019. **34**(1): p. 54–59.

100. Hebert, R., et al., *Positive and negative religious coping and well-being in women with breast cancer.* J Palliat Med, 2009. **12**(6): p. 537–45.

101. Pargament, K., et al., *God help me: religious coping efforts as predictors of the outcomes to significant negative life events.* Am J Community Psychol, 1990. **18**: p. 793–24.

102. Pargament, K., et al., *Religion and the Problem-Solving Process: Three Styles of Coping.* JSSR, 1988. **27**(1): p. 90–104.

103. Kemper, K.J. and S.C. Danhauer, *Music as therapy.* South Med J, 2005. **98**(3): p. 282–8.

104. Rauscher, F.H., et al., *Music and spatial task performance.* Nature, 1993. **365**(6447): p. 611.

105. Rauscher, F.H., et al., *Improved maze learning through early music exposure in rats.* Neurol Res, 1998. **20**(5): p. 427–32.

ACKNOWLEDGEMENTS

Thank you Marianne Tatepo for believing in me and giving me the opportunity to write this book. Your vision has shaped this manuscript, and this body of work wouldn't have been possible without your dedication, efforts and talent.

I am grateful to Becky Alexander, the brilliant copy-editor of this book. Thank you for your careful and thoughtful review of this manuscript, and for your very helpful feedback.

I would also like to thank Craig Brierley, Tom Parkhill and Matt Warren for giving me my first chances.

As I was working on this book and needed an instant mood fix, I often turned to my father's music to recharge. The songs he creates uplifted and energized me during the writing process.

Finally, a huge thanks to the entire team at Happy Place/Ebury Books, including Anna Bowen, Ellie Crisp, Fearne Cotton. I am so excited to be part of the Penguin family.